# ~~DIFFICULT~~ aging in place conversations

what industry experts have to say

*Adrienne Mintz*
*678-522-1922*

Members of
**The National Aging in Place Council**

No part of this publication may be reproduced, stored in a retrieval system, or transmitted in any form or by any means—electronic, photocopying, recording, or otherwise—without prior written permission, except in the case of brief excerpts in critical reviews and articles. For permission requests, contact NAIPC@AgeInPlace.org.

All rights reserved.

Copyright © 2023 National Aging in Place Council

ISBN: 978-1-59094-261-1

The author disclaims responsibility for adverse effects or consequences from the misapplication or injudicious use of the information contained in this book. Mention of resources and associations does not imply an endorsement.

# Table of Contents

## INTRODUCTION

**We Need to Talk**
By Steve Gurney..................................................................3

**Facilitating Difficult Conversations**
By Deanne O'Rear Cameron...................................................5

**Proactive Planning and Adaptation:**
**The Keys to Successful Aging and Thriving vs. Surviving**
By Catherine L. Owens........................................................11

## HOUSING

**Now Comes the Time to Talk About a Move**
By Diana Ahlf....................................................................23

**When to Declutter and Downsize**
By Ellen Goodwin...............................................................33

**Stubborn Parents in an Aging House With Worried Family:**
**Can We Find the Right Words?**
By Fritzi Gros-Daillon..........................................................43

**Home Safety Tips**
By Pam Santoro..................................................................53

**Some Dynamics of Home Accessibility Decisions**
    By Louis Tenenbaum ................................................................63

## HEALTHCARE

**Addressing Urinary Incontinence**
    By Colleen Bather ....................................................................73

**Navigating a Life Changing Diagnosis**
    By Tricia Bell ............................................................................83

**End-of-Life Wishes**
    By Ronnie Genser .....................................................................93

**Surgery and Older Adults**
    By Mathius Marc Gertz ..........................................................101

**Discussing Housing, Treatment, and Care Options With a Loved One After a Difficult Diagnosis**
    By Gina LaPalio-Lakin ...........................................................109

**Medication Matters**
    By Gretchen (Gigi) Marquardt ...............................................125

**"How Can I Get My Mom to Use Her Walker?"**
    By Courtney Nalty ..................................................................139

**Receiving and Accepting a Dementia Diagnosis**
    By Courtney Nalty ..................................................................145

**"Am I Really Ready for Joint Replacement Surgery?"**
    By David T. Neuman .............................................................151

## FINANCE & FAMILY

**When is the Right Time to Claim Social Security?**
    By Tara Ballman .....................................................................163

**The Probate Process as it Relates to Real Estate**
    By Peter Demidovich.................................................................175

**The Use of Home Equity in Retirement**
    By Sue Haviland......................................................................187

**Aging Solo**
    By Carolyn Novotny ...............................................................197

## TRANSPORTATION & TRAVEL

**When is it Time to Take Away the Keys?**
    By Melanie Henry....................................................................209

**What if You Die When Traveling?**
    By Helen Scherrer-Diamond ...................................................223

## SOCIAL ISSUES

**Older Adults With Special Needs Children**
    By Peter Klamkin ....................................................................233

**Cultural Considerations as Your Loved One Ages**
    By Jennifer Lagemann .............................................................241

**Deciding Who Will Take Care of Your Elderly Family Members**
    By Wayne Mitchell...................................................................249

**Protecting Privacy**
    By Heather Nickerson .............................................................257

**Getting Help for Difficult People**
    By Jennifer Prell ......................................................................265

**Being Prepared**
    By Kelly Rogers .......................................................................271

**Resources**
   Aging Acronyms and Glossary..................................................275

# Introduction

ON BEHALF OF the members of the National Aging in Place Council (NAIPC), I'd like to thank you for taking time to research the products, services, and resources available to help you, your friends, and your loved ones successfully age in place.

Creating an aging in place plan does not necessarily mean a plan to stay in your current home until you die. Situations change. Medical diagnoses occur. Sometimes it may be necessary to make a change to your residence; other times, you may be able to make alterations to your current lifestyle to remain in place.

Either way, home is where you lay your head. And aging in place is really about making your current home—preferably the home of your choosing—and lifestyle as comfortable, safe, and secure as long as possible. And if circumstances may change, you have a plan for your next home to be comfortable, safe, and secure as long as possible.

The members of NAIPC want you to be aware of all your options at every stage in the process. If you begin planning early, the options from which you may choose are much greater than those available in a crisis mode.

For nearly two decades, NAIPC members have been trusted advisors for families seeking resources and individuals creating their own aging in place plans. Our mission is focused on bringing education and resources to communities in what we call the five pillars of aging: housing, health & wellness, finance, transportation, and social engagement.

If you have any questions as you read this book or at any time in your aging in place journey, feel free to reach out to NAIPC at naipc@ageinplace.org or visit www.ageinplace.org.

Tara Ballman

Executive Director, NAIPC

# We Need to Talk

## By Steve Gurney
*Founder of Positive Aging Community*

MY DAD FELL. My mom's car has mysterious scratches. Money is missing from my loved one's account. My friend has a terminal diagnosis and limited resources. Aging in place brings many difficult situations. What do you do as a caregiver or loved one? Who can you trust? Simple. The people who have already lived these situations. The people who have said, "We need to talk," and are now ready to tell us about it.

This book is unique. It does not contain checklists or to-do lists. It doesn't feature theories from scientists or prescriptive advice from doctors or academics. This is a book of lived wisdom—a book of hard conversations and arduous lessons learned. The purpose of this collection of questions and answers is to dive into the complex and sensitive discussions that surround aging in place.

How we define "aging in place" is subjective. Where and how we want to age is an intensely personal decision. Not surprisingly, conversations about aging in place can be emotionally charged, filled with uncertainty, and tinged with conflict. They can also be liberating.

By planning for "aging in place," we can create an opportunity for ourselves or our loved ones to live in an environment they choose with dignity and purpose. Any conversation about aging in place requires compassion, understanding, and an open mind—on both sides.

While checklists and workbooks can be helpful to guide us on an "aging in place" journey, what is most important is having conversations with individuals in your network—including family members and providers.

Whether you are an adult child concerned about the well-being of your aging parents, a professional caregiver attempting to strike the delicate balance between independence and safety, or an older adult grappling with the idea of relinquishing control, this book serves as a guide to help you navigate these challenging discussions.

Drawing from personal experiences, research, and expert advice, "Difficult Aging in Place Conversations" offers practical strategies and insights for approaching sensitive topics such as health and care needs, financial considerations, home modifications, and end-of-life planning. It provides a roadmap to foster effective communication, establish boundaries, and make informed decisions that honor the desires and dignity of all involved.

Throughout these pages, you will discover stories of resilience, compassion, and love. You will gain a deeper understanding of the emotional complexities that arise when confronting the realities of aging. Most importantly, you will find a renewed sense of hope and possibility. We hope you finish this book knowing that difficult conversations can be transformative and lead to growth, connection, and the creation of meaningful solutions.

Join us on this insightful exploration of "Difficult Aging in Place Conversations." We hope this book serves as a catalyst for compassionate dialogue, healing, and stronger relationships. Talking, listening, and talking some more is, after all, the best way to make a plan for aging in place.

# Facilitating Difficult Conversations
## By Deanne O'Rear-Cameron

DIFFICULT CONVERSATIONS ARE an inevitable part of life. Whether it's addressing a sensitive topic with a loved one, discussing a disagreement, or confronting a challenging situation, the ability to facilitate these conversations with empathy, openness, and respect is crucial. While these discussions may be uncomfortable, they also provide an opportunity for growth, understanding, and resolution. Let's explore some effective strategies and techniques to help you navigate difficult conversations with grace and the proper mindset to foster positive outcomes.

Prepare: Before engaging in a difficult conversation, preparing yourself emotionally and mentally is essential. Take time to reflect on your feelings, biases, and triggers related to the topic. Recognize that your perspective may not be the only valid one and be open to different viewpoints. By understanding your own emotions and biases, you can approach the conversation with a calmer and more objective mindset. Each person's perspective is past programming in the mind that is based on prior experiences, other people's experiences they have heard, and many other influences. This is why going into the conversation with an open mind is key.

Choose the Right Setting: Timing and environment play a crucial role in the success of difficult conversations. Select a location that is neutral and free from distractions, ensuring privacy and minimizing interruptions thus keeping the mind focused on what is being discussed. Additionally, consider the timing of the conversation. Avoid discussing sensitive matters when either party is feeling exhausted, stressed, or preoccupied. Find a time when both parties can dedicate their full attention and energy to the discussion. This will allow the conversation to flow more positively and constructively.

Practice Conscious Listening: Conscious listening is a fundamental skill in facilitating difficult conversations. Give the person speaking your undivided attention, maintain eye contact, and use non-verbal cues to convey your interest and understanding. Focus on understanding the person's perspective rather than formulating your response. Reflecting and paraphrasing their words can demonstrate empathy and ensure that you have accurately understood their viewpoint. Be careful not to overlook this important part. If you are not actively listening to their why and perspectives on the subject being discussed it may make the outcome and resolution more difficult to achieve.

Express Empathy and Compassion: Empathy and compassion are powerful tools in difficult conversations. Validate the emotions and experiences of the other person by acknowledging their feelings. Use phrases like, "I understand this is challenging for you" or "I can see why you feel that way." Demonstrating empathy creates a safe space for open dialogue and shows that you genuinely care about their perspective, even if you don't agree. Be mindful of the fact that we all want to know the person we are speaking with actually cares for our well-being.

Use "I" Statements: When expressing your thoughts and feelings, using "I" statements can be more effective than placing blame or making accusatory statements. For example, saying, "I feel hurt when you do this" instead of "You always do this" can prevent the conversation from becoming defensive or confrontational. You will promote a more constructive and collaborative atmosphere.

Look for Common Ground: Identify areas of agreement or shared values during the conversation. By highlighting common ground, you can build a foundation for finding solutions or compromises. Look for shared goals or interests that can serve as a basis for finding a mutually beneficial outcome. Recognizing shared objectives can help both parties work together to reach a resolution or understanding. This can help with future conversations as well since you have already identified common ground and strengthened the relationship.

Practice Emotional Control: Difficult conversations can provoke strong emotions. It is crucial to remain calm and composed during the discussion. If you find yourself becoming overwhelmed or reactive, take a moment to breathe deeply and regain your composure. Emotionally charged reactions can hinder effective communication and derail the conversation by putting the person on the defensive. By practicing emotional regulation, you can maintain a constructive and respectful dialogue for everyone involved.

Focus on Solutions: Instead of dwelling on the challenge or assigning blame, shift the conversation towards finding solutions. Encourage brainstorming and creative thinking to explore alternative perspectives and potential resolutions. Keep the focus on the future and what can be done to address the issue at hand. Working collaboratively towards finding solutions fosters a sense of shared responsibility and promotes a positive outcome.

Facilitating difficult conversations requires intention, empathy, mindfulness to understand the perspectives of everyone who is involved in the conversation, and a commitment to respectful communication. By preparing yourself, practicing active listening, expressing empathy, and seeking common ground, you can navigate these conversations with grace and an open mind. Remember that difficult conversations are an opportunity for growth, understanding, and strengthening relationships. With these strategies in mind, you can approach challenging discussions with confidence and foster positive outcomes.

## Deanne O'Rear-Cameron

DEANNE IS A Professional Mindset Development Specialist, Aging in Place Advocate, Speaker, and Author.

Deanne started her journey in Human/Mindset Development and Management Training over 30 years ago. Her passion is to help everyone thrive Personally and Professionally. She embodies what she teaches and helps people from all walks of life to find their true identity and create a life by design.

After working in the Older Adult Industry over the last decade and a half, she developed a program for Understanding the Mindset of Older Adults and a program for Professional and Family Caregivers. This has allowed her to bring together her passions.

Deanne serves as the Chairperson for the City of Las Vegas Senior Citizens Advisory Board, Chair of the Board of Directors of the National Aging in Place Council bringing a local chapter to Southern NV, Member of the Commission on Aging for Nevada, and Chair of the Seniors and Law Enforcement Together Council.

Deanne is also an entertainer alongside her husband, Sythe.

**Linkedin:**

https://www.linkedin.com/in/deanne-orear-cameron/

**Website:**

YouTube: http://www.youtube.com/user/deanneorearcameron

# Proactive Planning and Adaptation: The Keys to Successful Aging and Thriving vs. Surviving

By Catherine L. Owens

IT WAS THE summer of 2020, during the height of the Covid pandemic, when I received a call from Joan. It had been a year since she sold her home and moved to an independent living apartment in a Continuing Care Retirement Community (CCRC). Because she believed in taking a proactive approach to planning, Joan understood the importance of living in a home and environment conducive to current needs, along with potential care needs. As difficult as selling her beloved home was, she was ready to live in a home and community where her inability to continue driving would not limit her from staying active and engaging with others. Shortly after moving, her daughter commented on how much happier she seemed, which surprised Joan. As she contemplated her daughter's comment, she realized how her inability to drive had impacted her life in ways she had not really considered. Joan admitted her daughter was right. Not only was she happier, but she also loved feeling a sense of community again, always having something to look forward to, and continual opportunities to share her time and talents with others.

As our conversation continued, I could feel Joan's pride, and almost see her smile and eyes light up, as she spoke of her successful and rewarding career as an educator, social worker, and mental health professional.

There was laughter and undeniable joy as she reminisced, sharing stories of a life well lived and memories she held dear to her heart. Then came a long moment of silence. I will never forget sitting in my office on the phone with her, feeling her smile fade away as the joy and laughter in her voice was replaced with sadness and tears. Joan confided the difficulty she was having recognizing the lively, vibrant, full of zest for life, woman she had always been. *Stay in place orders* for the city were lifting, yet state sanctioned isolation protocols for care communities, Joan's included, remained out of safety concerns for residents and staff. FaceTime, video chats, and peering through windows of a home continued to be the norm.

In most states, independent living communities are not licensed to provide care or governed by the same state residential care regulations and laws related to assisted living and memory care communities. Although Joan's home was in the independent living area of the community, she was in a community where all levels of care were provided, causing the independent living residents to fall under the same state mandated safety protocols set in place for care communities.

Along with mandated and well-intentioned safety protocols came the awareness of the negative impacts those measures were having on a person's overall physical, mental, and emotional well-being. Isolation had a significant impact on older adults and family members unable to physically visit one another. For Joan, extended isolation orders only magnified the suffering she was experiencing from lack of social engagement and human connections. Joan felt she had gone from thriving to surviving.

Realizing her home and environment could no longer meet her current needs, Joan decided something had to change. She wondered if stand-alone independent living communities without additional levels of care were required to follow the same state mandated safety protocols set in place for care communities. With curiosity, and a bit of renewed hope, Joan began making phone calls.

When you hear the term "Aging in Place," what comes to mind? Although the meaning can vary for people, an overall accepted reference for the term "Aging in Place" is staying in our home through end-of-life.

If you were to search the term "Aging in Place," you would find the following definition, or something similar.

*"Aging in Place" refers to the ability of an older person <u>to live</u> in their own home or community <u>safely, independently, and comfortably</u> as they age. It involves modifying the living environment and accessing necessary services to meet the changing needs of older adults. The goal of aging in place is to enable older adults <u>to maintain their autonomy, dignity, and quality of life</u> by providing the support they need to remain in their homes and communities for as long as possible.*

*This concept emphasizes the importance of proactive planning and adaptation to ensure older adults can continue to live fulfilling lives as they age.*

Staying in our home through the end-of-life is a natural and desirable goal, and for many, this mindset and approach is the only considered and acceptable option as we grow through our older years. Consistent with the definition above, as a society, health industry, and individuals, we often associate maintaining independence, dignity, and quality of life in our older years, with the term aging in place (staying in our homes through end-of-life).

Along with what we have come to define as Aging in Place are common feelings and emotions evoked when discussing the concept for both older adults and their loved ones. Feelings and emotions one may wish to avoid, or be unaware of, can hinder a person's ability to approach and/or facilitate difficult conversations as age-related needs and concerns arise. Consider the following questions:

## DIFFICULT AGING IN PLACE CONVERSATIONS

- How do you or a loved one feel when hearing the term "Aging in Place"?
- Do you feel resolute in the idea that maintaining autonomy, dignity, and quality of life is only accomplished by staying in your home through the end-of-life?
- Are topics related to "Aging in Place" easy and comfortable for you to discuss or would you prefer to not think of or discuss such topics?

The above definition states, "*This concept emphasizes the importance of proactive planning and adaptation to ensure older adults can continue to live fulfilling lives as they age.*" Although I meet individuals like Joan who understand how proactive planning and adapting play a role in influencing positive quality of life outcomes as they age, the opposite approach is the common path I see taken. Through years of supporting families through difficult conversations and complex decisions, I have gained a deep awareness and unique understanding of common concepts, mindsets, emotions, social stigmas, and preconceived ideas that can create barriers when discussing and/or making necessary quality of life decisions. Discussions regarding proactive planning, adapting a home or changing an environment to align with current needs or situations, addressing potential declines in health and abilities, and need for support or care, are often avoided until an emergency presents. Many of which may have been avoided or decreased in severity had a mindset and approach of proactive planning and adaptability been considered, discussed, and taken.

The definition continues with, "*The goal of aging in place is to enable older adults to maintain their autonomy, dignity, and quality of life by providing the support they need to remain in their homes and communities for as long as possible.*"

## PROACTIVE PLANNING AND ADAPTATION

Where you live does matter, and at times due to circumstances or situations, adapting a current home or moving to a new home, may be the answer to *"maintaining autonomy, dignity, and quality of life."* Successful aging in place is not a linear approach or goal only related to later stages of life. It is approaching every stage of life with a mindset of proactive aging and wellness, focused on Putting in Place what we need to continue living safely, independently, and comfortably so we successfully age well in any place.

Think of the places you called home throughout various stages of your life. Whether it was moving to your first home, relocating for a job, settling down to raise a family, downsizing as kids grew, and every stage in between. Did your home or environment adapt or change depending on circumstances, needs, and plans for your life? Was the location or size based on needs or desired lifestyle with a goal of putting in place what would provide for the greatest quality of life during each phase of your life?

Why would we not adapt or change our home and environment based on needs or desired lifestyle in later stages of life, with the same goal of putting in place what would provide for the greatest quality of life possible? As we grow older, planning for situations, health needs, changes in abilities, and maintaining a mindset of putting in place what is needed for continued quality of life becomes even more important.

I met Rob while golfing when I was paired with him and his two friends who were looking for a fourth player. As the round of golf progressed, one of the players asked what my profession was. I revealed that a strong focus of my career was supporting older adults and families navigating complex, difficult, and often overwhelming discussions and decisions related to senior services and care. Rob commented that he wished he had met me the previous year when his elderly mother experienced a sudden decline in health. He shared the concerns he had in her ability to manage her large home, and how every time he tried to discuss the situation and viable solutions, he was met with, "I don't want to discuss this." Margie took extraordinary pride in her independence and preferred to be in control of making her own decisions.

Rob and his mother Margie enjoyed weekly lunch outings together. Rob chuckled as he talked of seeing his mother peeking out the window every week as she watched for his arrival. The smile on her face when he pulled into her driveway was something he always enjoyed and had become part of their weekly routine.

It was this time last year when he pulled into his mother's driveway for their lunch outing and noticed she was not sitting in her usual spot. A bit surprised and concerned, he went inside to check on his mother. Margie was actively experiencing a stroke. Rob took immediate action and upon receiving emergency medical care, Margie was admitted to the hospital. Three days later, Rob met with her care team and was told she would be discharged in 48 hours and was not safe living at home alone due to assistance she needed with Activities of Daily Living (ADLs). It was recommended she transition to an assisted living community, and he was given a list of local communities to call. In that moment Rob realized he had no idea where to begin, what he should consider when researching communities, and what other options were available to potentially support his mother to live safely in her home. The hardest part of all, he admitted, was having no idea what was important to his mother regarding these types of decisions. Because of her desire to maintain control, avoid such topics, and him not wanting to push difficult conversations with her, they were in a situation where she was unable to communicate her wishes and he was put in full control of making the best decision he could with what little he knew.

As I listened to Rob share of the journey he and his mom experienced, it made me think of how often families experience similar situations.

## Proactive Planning and Adaptation

Consider these statistics from the Administration for Community Living (acl.gov) about LTC:
- Someone turning 65 today has a 70% chance of needing long-term care services in their lifetime.
- One third of today's 65-year-olds may never need long-term care support—but 20% will need it longer than five years.
- Women typically need care longer than men. (3.7 years versus 2.2 years)[1]

Set aside the common definition of "Aging in Place." If you were to define what it means to you at your current and previous stages of life, what would it consist of?

Chances are, what defines each of those words would encompass a wide range of factors, often changing or evolving as you continue to grow, learn, experience, and transition through each stage of your life.

This book addresses common, yet rarely discussed topics surrounding potential needs and concerns with aging and how to facilitate the difficult conversations often associated with each topic. Approaching every stage of life with a mindset of proactive aging and wellness requires planning and adapting, especially at later stages of life. It may, at times, require uncomfortable and difficult conversations on topics we would rather avoid, but are critically important.

Having conversations, even difficult ones, about hopes and fears, what is important, potential concerns and necessary support, can help in recognizing where planning, adaptability, and proactive lifestyle choices may be needed. Putting in place what is needed allows for increased opportunity of living safely, independently, and comfortably with dignity, autonomy, and quality of life, and successfully aging well in any place.

---

[1] acl.gov/ltc/basic-needs/how-much-care-will-you-need

## Catherine L. Owens

CATHERINE L. OWENS is a nationally recognized Senior Living Industry expert, Aging Well authority, and owner of CLO Consulting. She is an internationally award-winning, best-selling author of the books *Shine on You Crazy Diamond: Even When Your Crown Feels Heavy* and *Be Your Own Hero: Senior Living Decisions Simplified* which she wrote to address the emotional and social aspects often hindering one's ability to make proactive, quality of life choices, and assist people in navigating senior living decisions.

For Catherine, the phrase *Be Your Own Hero* is not just the title of her book, *Be Your Own Hero: Senior Living Decisions Simplified*, it is a mindset that has resonated with her since childhood, embodies who she is, and an approach she takes in all aspects of life. Catherine's belief that everyone has the power and capability to *Be Their Own Hero*, is not only a common thread seen and felt in her personal and professional life,

## Proactive Planning and Adaptation

but what drives her motivation, desire, and commitment, to encourage, support, and empower others to find their own hero within.

As Co-Host of *The Tattered Capes Podcast*, Catherine is dedicated to changing the conversations around proactive healthy aging choices that hold potential for increased opportunity for continued higher quality of life as we age.

Catherine serves as a member of the Board of Directors for the National Aging in Place Council and is a recipient of the Tribute to Women and Industry (TWIN) Award which honors women who have excelled in their field and made significant contributions to their industry.

Catherine loves spending time with her family and enjoys kayaking, golf, and wildlife photography.

To learn more about Catherine, the services her company provides, and information about her award-winning books, visit www.catherinelowens.com.

# HOUSING

ROUSING

# Now Comes the Time to Talk About a Move

## By Diana Ahlf

**Question:**

WE ARE IN the process of relocating my parents into a smaller residence in an older adult community. They are both in agreement that it is time to find a more appropriate home, but I am worried about the mental and emotional stress this will put on them. Do you have suggestions on how we can safely transition them into their new home?

**Answer:**

We all knew this day was coming, we just didn't know when the time would come and how to handle all that is involved, correct?

This is a very common conversation heard by any senior specialist, whether it is a transition specialist, residency counselor, real estate agent, intake nurse, or social worker. Any family with aging parents will expect to go through this at some point. The dreaded point. Because it is hard.

Think of how hard it is for most people to make changes in life. Fear of making changes is on the top of the list of why people don't change jobs or circumstances even if it would improve their life. Now that your parents have decided it is time for the next chapter, we need to help them with the emotions of leaving their longtime home, the fear of the unknown, and adjusting to new people and experiences. The good news is with the right support, your parents will make it through just fine!

Like any other "big life" change, the first thing to do is to acknowledge the situation. You are already ahead of the game by recognizing this may be one of the biggest steps the folks have taken in a long time. They may have tossed this idea around for years before you even knew about it.

The first order of business is to talk to them about how proud you are that they are moving forward. Parents expect that they are always the ones uplifting and supporting their children, not the other way around. We find that when the family members verbally support their parents, the decision solidifies in the parents' minds.

That is not to say there will not be second thoughts or doubts. We would encourage keeping in mind to "stay the course" and "keep your eye on the prize." That way when there is a setback, you are not thrown off and let them throw in the towel. We would suggest having a knee-jerk reaction ready to deliver, such as telling them it's all going to be ok in the end. You won't have to think on your feet, you will be prepared.

Case example: Bobby and Cathy kept their lives quiet from their 5 adult children. When Cathy took a hard fall and Bobby became overwhelmed and fearful of diminishing health for the both of them, they knew it was time. Their children were surprised they weren't involved in that conversation but backed them up solidly.

Several issues came up along the way: What do we do with all our belongings? What if we miss our friends? Each time, one or more of the children would gently remind them that this was an excellent decision on their part, everything was going to be ok, we will help you work through this and find resources to guide us.

Amber, their granddaughter, even calmed them down by helping them get as much as they could get accomplished each day...and then stop. You can only do what you can do, she told them. Bobby and Cathy allowed themselves to be helped and were grateful their children participated in this transition and because of that, not only did they

## NOW COMES THE TIME TO TALK ABOUT A MOVE

*(handwritten at top: relocation: Certified Senior Advisor)*

move to their manageable apartment more fluidly, but the family grew closer in the process.

The next step is <u>preparedness for some set-back situations</u>. Transitioning older adults into their next chapter has many moving parts. If they have talked to you about moving from their current home, it's likely they have talked to their friends. Maybe they have visited communities they are considering. Understand that they may not qualify financially for their top pick. We see this in the industry all too often. The razzle dazzle commercials, the beautiful entry fountain, the friendly tour, the steak dinner. The senior envisions living there and then learns that they don't qualify.

To address this, it could be time to look into resourcing an agency that does the work of relocation for you. This is called a <u>Certified Senior Advisor</u>. They take all the information of matters such as assets, income including: interest dividends, social security, annuities, VA benefits, pensions, disability benefits. This information is then coupled with the interests of the senior. Maybe dad still likes to play golf and a nearby residency is close to a familiar course. Maybe mom can't be too far from her beloved church. The counselor then narrows down the field so that any community they tour will work out financially. The service is free. The agency is paid a commission from the residency, it's built into their budget in fact.

Case example: Don and Marge have worked very hard to build their financial portfolio. They realize independent living is not cheap, but they want a beautiful place to call home when they move. Marge has a flair for decorating and is looking forward to making a home she can showcase to her friends. They visit and fall in love with a prestigious senior residency. They pick out their dream apartment and prepare to get their home ready to market. The residency counselor calls them and tells them that after the actuary ran their numbers, they can qualify for the 1-bedroom, smaller apartment vs. the one they had their hearts set on. They are, of course, very disappointed to say the least. A friend recommended calling a Certified Senior Advisor, which is free of charge to them. They met with the advisor and come to find that they could in fact afford a place in an area they didn't even know about. They ended up getting an even nicer place with large windows, a golf course view, and soaring ceilings which afforded Marge an even better decorating opportunity to enjoy. They are very happy it worked out this way!

Another circumstance we see is when a friend or family member has promised for years to buy the home, but when a fair price is addressed, the situation falls apart. The family member had in their minds that the house is worth less, or they expected a "price break" because of the relationship.

This can throw the folks off course, as they weren't prepared to hire a real estate broker and go into the open market. With the real estate market changing every day, the most important advice is to hire a full-time broker who is an SRES specialist, and who is a good-standing member in the NAIPC organization.

SRES is an acronym for Senior Real Estate Specialist. These folks are held to the gold standard of helping seniors. It is their specialization. The National Association of Realtors has deemed it to be a designation requiring education and testing. A good-standing member of the NAIPC is important because it is an additional layer to the broker's identity who has built authority to their discipline. The NAIPC requires a vetting process with a background check. You are receiving service from the best of the best full-time real estate agent because they have their finger on the pulse of the ever-changing market. Every market is different, and it is crucial that the Realtor you are working with has the best handle on the situation. Every dollar counts and a part time agent could unknowingly leave money on the table. We don't want that!

Case example: Susan's niece has been telling her aunt that "when the time comes, I want to take over the family house and buy it from you, Aunt Susan." After Susan selects her independent living facility, Susan calls her niece and tells her she's ready to talk about selling the house to her at X price (fair market value, maybe minus a couple of bucks). 2 days goes by with no further word. The niece has her dad call Susan and confesses that they never spoke to a qualified lender and now she isn't qualified for that price and would she please reduce it to a lesser amount (less than fair market value).

Susan explains that her proceeds are qualifying her into the residence, and she can't reduce the price. Susan researches her local real estate market and finds a full-time SRES who is also an NAIPC member. The real estate specialist knows exactly what to do to accomplish Susan's goals of getting her the most amount of money in the shortest amount of time with the least amount of stress. The home goes on the open market and Susan is most pleased to find she was able to get the help she needed while partnering with this agent. She made more off the sale than she anticipated, which gave her some "play money" and bought herself some new furniture for her lovely new home.

For anyone, particularly an older adult, the fear of the unknown can be overwhelming. "What if I don't fit in?" is a very common fear, whether a person admits it or not. "How do I know if I will really like it there?" is another. We would continue with the encouraging conversations about why this is the best thing to do at this time. Remind them on the "why's" of specific reasons they selected a particular home or residency. Maybe it has a pool they can't wait to get into, maybe it's their view in their apartment. Whatever the high points are, reinforce them. Good reminders are a great remedy to overcoming doubt.

Case example: Jim and Mary selected a senior residency that a family member recommended. As the intake process begins, Mary begins feeling nagging doubts that she would be able to make new friends of similar interests. She worries that there will be "cliques" that will snub her. Jim and their son listened to her concerns. They called the residency and asked that the "ambassador" that is normally assigned to new residents to make them feel at home faster after the big move, meet with Mary and show her the ropes now. The ambassador is a person who lives there, loves it, and knows how to find the right groups such as dancing, bible study, Wii gaming, book groups, social clubs, even karaoke and stand-up comedian night groups. They then introduce Mary into her groups of interest, and she makes new friends. By the time they do move in, she already knows people who welcome her into their group. She's very into Wii gaming, much to Jim's surprise and delight. Mary was named "rookie of the year" by fellow members.

Sometimes even with the decision made and everything falling into place, people become overwhelmed by the process of all their stuff acquired over the years. This could be severe enough to cause them to pause or even chicken out of what they know they need to do, which is get out from under it and move.

At that point, we recommend hiring a transitioning company, again vetted by NAIPC, to make the transaction as safe and smooth as possible. The company has a plan in place to arrange for selling unwanted items. (They have experts at knowing values of items and how to best negotiate for the best price.) They design a layout for the senior's new home, so we don't bring too much, but keeping in mind the senior has their own valued treasures that make their new place home.

Case example: For years, Christine has been worried about her mom's safety in a big 2-story home with dangerous stairs. Her mother, Mary, argues that she's just fine and besides, what in the world would we do with all my belongings. Christine suggests an estate sale, but Mary says she's heard they scalp you and shortchange you in the end.

## Professional Transitioning Expert
### Now Comes the Time to Talk About a Move

A friend of Christine's hears about a company that is vetted by an organization that demands performance from its members. Christine convinces her mom to at least meet the Professional Transitioning Expert. When the representative comes to the house with a very organized plan to move Mary into her new place with the items Mary has decided to bring, both mother and daughter breathe a sigh of relief.

The Transitioning Expert then moves her team into action, sorting, boxing, and cleaning. They also make some repairs that are needed to render the best price for Mary's sale of the home. She has a dangerous staircase that needs to be made safe for showings. She has rotting drywall with probable mold in the garage that needs to be removed. Some simple updates that don't break the bank are all accomplished in a very short amount of time. All done by the team. A working machine of sorts with each person on the team taking care of their individual responsibility.

Mary and Christine are so pleased that Mary has been safely transitioned into a beautiful downtown unit with all the amenities she could hope for. Mary is grateful her daughter cared enough about her to help her out of the unsafe situation. They enjoy a weekly Target run together now. What fun!

As we progress through this time with our loved ones, let's not lose sight that there is a beginning, a middle, and an end to every story. Good and bad stories all have endings. If we are supportive and do our best, we will be proud of our own selves. Those of us who take care of older adults have a special joy that is not trumpeted by the crowds. And we know that we have done a good job and done the right thing!

## Diana Ahlf

DIANA AHLF IS an award-winning Re/Max agent who specializes in compassionately helping seniors. She's a life-long Chicago area resident and one of six children who learned the art of negotiation and fair play early on.

Diana knew real estate was her passion even while studying at DuPage College as she worked after school in a construction trailer handing out new home brochures. There her real estate career began as she passionately absorbed all she could about home sales and new construction and quickly moved from a successful sales agent to the youngest manager Cambridge Homes ever had. Diana's dedication won her Sales Manager of the Year of the entire Chicago region in her first managing year.

In 2008, Diana switched gears from new construction and gave her all to residential real estate. In her first year, she won the coveted "Rising

Star" award working with Re/Max, the largest and finest real estate company in the world.

Diana found she greatly enjoyed working with seniors the year she helped her mother-in-law move from St. Charles to Friendship Village. It was then she found a welcome place for her skill and compassion and has since delighted in prioritizing seniors as her #1 goal. Her genuine kindness has made many long-term friendships along the way.

Realizing there were so many scams targeting our seniors, Diana worked on her SRES designation. A SRES is the only designation that is designed to ensure the individual agent has specialized training to guide the seller into their next, and maybe, final chapter. Diana lovingly works with all sellers and buyers, and her senior specialty is near and dear to her heart.

# When to Declutter and Downsize
## By Ellen Goodwin

**Question:**

MY PARENTS ARE in their 70s and happily living at home, but I'm worried about what happens if this abruptly changes. They have 40+ years of stuff at home that makes them happy but could present safety and logistical challenges, in case of a move, at any moment. What are some strategies I can use to bring this up with them so they can get out ahead of it?

**Answer:**

The "why" behind a decision to declutter and/or downsize isn't always about bringing joy, saving money, or adding rainbow-colored, eye-pleasing storage solutions. At Artifcts, when adult children ask us questions relating to helping their parents to declutter and downsize, we hear a mix of anxiety and love in the asking.

The anxiety is about the reality of all that stuff and the risks it can create and, ultimately, the time and cost to manage moving it all. The love is out of respect for their parents' autonomy, way of life, and attachment to their belongings. It's *their* stuff!

I know. I am facing this challenge myself with my parents, and I am leaning on the wisdom of professional gerontologists, neurologists, senior move managers, and even Arti Community members to guide me through this conversation and process.

## My Tale

Throughout my childhood, my mother brought us along to garage and estate sales and the occasional consignment shop with stern, "Don't touch!" admonishments. Our home took on the feel of a country bed and breakfast. My mother's artistic eye wove together family heirlooms and new (to us) items she picked up along the way for a cozy, welcoming feel.

She ushered in each new season with a change in the décor. She would carefully pack the knickknacks and wall art away with my dad's help, dust off those in waiting, and, voilà, the house took on a whole new feel.

Less often touched was the sewing room where our family's history was on display. Fabrics for Halloween costumes, quilts, bonnets (yes, really, bonnets!) folded up and at the ready, as well as bits and bops for random school projects and plays. Since the nearest craft store was a 30-minute drive and both of my parents worked, popping out for project materials on a school night was out of the question.

My parents left each of the three of us to our own devices where our bedrooms were concerned. We didn't tend to accumulate much anyway, or so we thought. As we went off to college and it was time to repurpose those rooms, the Smurf drums, doll houses, magazines, special outfits, and childhood collections did actually fill most of the upstairs closet space.

The simple reality was that in a two-story, 2,500 sq. ft. old farmhouse, the storage that was available was filled, attic and basement included. But isn't that the norm? It's the same premise by which people often argue against expanding a major highway from four lanes to six – more lanes, more traffic. More storage, more stuff.

So as my parents begin enjoying their 70s, I too must have these conversations to prepare for the inevitable that could be years or decades away. It's not easy. They have the storage. They can blissfully ignore what's tucked away behind closed doors and live happily. Until they can't.

That's why we're here now, to talk about strategies for this type of "Difficult Conversation."

> *If you read nothing else, read this:*
> *Have the conversation now!*

Today, if possible. Make the time. Rushing this conversation or saving it until the 11th hour creates nothing but problems. The biggest problem comes down to the loss of control, the control being your parents', that is, and the havoc that can create in relationships.

Never forget it's their "stuff," and it's their home. Yes, you grew up there. Yes, it may be where you all still reunite on major holidays. But it is *their* home—these are *their* choices. The choices may seem irrational or impractical, but if they do no actual harm, physically or financially, you might need to swallow your words and preferences, and simply support them.

## Rushed and Ill-Timed Conversations Cost Time and Money

As the adult child, you're likely juggling some combination of family, work, community, and other life obligations of your own. You may not even live near your parents. Taking time out if a move becomes an emergency could cause you lost time (and maybe pay) at work, create logistical problems on your home front, and put you in a more... challenging mood to help.

When time is against your parents, they won't be able to sort through their belongings thoughtfully to decide what to donate, sell, pass down, and maybe recycle. And for items with financial value, your parent(s) will not have the time needed to find the right outlets and/or top bidders to sell them, forgoing income that might be important to their future plans and/or quality of life.

During a downsizing move, there may also be additional financial costs for a late move in/out, storage if they didn't get through it all, and moving stuff that won't even fit or is later tossed or re-homed after further reflection.

And of course, once an item is gone, it's gone. You could have at least commemorated it with a photo, a story, or, better yet, an Artifct, if only you had the time.

## Rushed and Ill-Timed Conversations Increase Guilt, Anxiety, and Stress

When time is against us, our better instincts and self-control take backseats to expediency.

The pressure of the clock naturally makes us, the adult children, more prone to push decisions upon our parents that are exactly the opposite of the kind, respectful approach we surely mean to take. No one needs raging guilt because we've failed to honor their memories and stories as we pushed our parents into letting go of their lifelong possessions, their comforts of home, their memories in the form of objects.

The ticking clock and rushed choices are also particularly dangerous for those with dementia. It's called "transfer trauma" and is more acute for those leaving their lifelong homes. Rushing a change of environment is stressful and can be detrimental to their wellbeing, including declines in physical, mental, behavioral, and functional well-being, according to a comprehensive review of 13 studies published in the *Gerontologist* and available from the US National Institute of Health (https://pubmed.ncbi.nlm.nih.gov/29718293/).

## Conversation Starters

Practically speaking, the best conversation starter for you will depend on your relationship with your parents. Do you only talk once a year? Or are you a regular for Sunday dinner, and you're highly aware of their daily lives and future plans?

No matter your relationship, never forget who you are: their kid! Even if you are an expert in move management, downsizing, and/or decluttering, *you are still their kid*. Parental and familial dynamics cannot be divorced from what can be a highly emotionally charged task. Don't be afraid to lean on others to help you through. Consider these conversations starters:

**Start #1: Help them discover and articulate what items matter most. Listen and learn.**

*Have you seen the TV show Legacy List with Matt Paxton? They tell these amazing family and community histories through objects they have in their homes. Paxton calls it a Legacy List, and everyone gets five items. What would be your five legacy list items?*

**Starter #2: Offer a plausible, relevant scenario and ask what they would do.**

I recently bought my 13-year-old daughter tickets to her first concert as a birthday surprise. Before giving her the tickets, I said, "Can you imagine how cool it must be to go to that concert?! If you could go to a concert like that and take anyone with you, who would you pick?"

It's no different here. My friend in Boston moved from 2,500 sq. ft. house to an 800 sq. ft. condo, and her dining table doesn't even fit in her new place. She figured this out after she moved. So frustrating. What items would be your "musts" for a big move?

**Starter #3: Go for the low hanging fruit.**

Mom, Dad, I'm worried that someday you'll want to move or downsize and there's just so much here to go through. I don't want it to become a major stress on you or any of us. I don't want it all tossed in a dumpster either. I'd like to help. And then offer some options, for example:
- I know it frustrates you that you aren't able to access what is in those top cupboards in the utility room. I have some time this weekend. Maybe we could start there, and I could pull out what's in it and together we could sort through it all. I'm happy to take items you don't want any more to {donation / consignment ...}.
- Do you want to pick a few spots for us to go through together and sort through? We could start with a single drawer in the living room bookcase or another spot you prefer.

**Starter #4: Talk about your real concerns for their health and safety. They may start to see their stuff differently.**

I am so grateful that you are both healthy and safe and happily living here. But I worry about your safety here in the long-term. I know that even that kitchen rug, if the corner gets turned up, could become a tripping hazard. Or if you don't clear off the entry table, your hand could slip if you lean on it. There's so much furniture in the living room that it's hard to maneuver safely. Maybe we could store the third side chair upstairs for now and bring it out when you need it?

## Let Me Know How It Goes – I'll Do the Same

My mother is a collector, as I have told you. I am forever, in my own mind, the opposite. As a child, I would declutter her drawers, recipe boxes, and baskets without permission. She was constantly checking the trash to see what I'd gotten when she wasn't looking.

Only through building Artifcts does she now trust me in her space again. She knows I'll honor her choices and belongings and listen to her stories, now and into the future via Artifcts.

No matter how you and your parents choose to sort through it all, make sure to choose a method to the madness that you agree upon together.

Here are few sources that have helped me and may help you along the way, too:

**Books*:* Keep the Memories, Lose the Stuff, by Matt Paxton, is a useful guide and highly relatable.

**Home service providers:** Companies like Forever Home help people to adapt their home environments to their changing needs as they age.

**Move managers:** Take the pressure off and find a local senior move manager. The National Association of Senior & Specialty Move Managers ensures certification, continuing education, insurance, and strict adherence to a code of ethics for its member companies.

**Online resources:** For more general information, opportunities, and inspiration about livable communities, try this free newsletter from AARP.

## Ellen Goodwin

ELLEN GOODWIN IS THE Co-founder and Chief Solutions Office fo Artifcts. Mother to a young teen, wife to a cyclist (and a cyclist herself), and lover of books, travel, and attempts at beautifying her home and garden. Prior to co-founding Artifcts, Ellen was the Chief Solutions Officer for a global data technology company. Ellen volunteers with her daughter through the National Charity League.

**Business website**

Artifcts.com

**LinkedIn**

https://www.linkedin.com/in/ellenlgoodwin/

# Stubborn Parents in an Aging House With Worried Family Can We Find the Right Words?

By Fritzi Gros-Daillon

**Question:**

MY PARENTS HAVE LIVED in their home for so long, and they are comfortable there. But their health is declining, and the house doesn't seem like the safest place for them to live anymore. They are stubborn and don't want to leave. What can we do? How can we talk with them to help them see that there are better options for them? What should we say to make this easier for them?

**Answer:**

Harold and Mary have been living in their cozy home for over 40 years. Nestled on a quiet street, their house stood as a testament to the life they had built together. The faded white paint on the exterior walls told stories of countless summers spent tending to the garden and hosting neighborhood barbeques. The front porch, adorned with a weathered wooden rocking chair, bore witness to the years of evenings spent watching the sunset and sipping tea.

Inside, the house reflected Harold and Mary's love and dedication. The living room boasted a worn-out, but oh-so-comfortable couch, surrounded by shelves filled with cherished photo albums, displaying the milestones of their family's journey. The scent of freshly baked cookies often wafted from the kitchen where Mary would stand at the worn wooden countertop, passing down family recipes to her children and grandchildren.

The walls of the hallway were adorned with framed artwork, created by their children when they were young, a colorful reminder of the joy and creativity that once filled the house. The staircase, worn and creaky, held the memories of children's laughter, music, and the aroma of a barbeque.

However, as Harold and Mary entered their late 70s, the signs of aging began to take a toll on them. Harold's once steady hands now trembled slightly as he tried to fix the leaky faucets and repair the aging roof. Mary's once keen eyesight started to blur, making it difficult for her to navigate the dimly lit rooms and her hearing began to fade, leaving her a bit disconnected from the world she knew so well. Even that sense of balance, once a reliable companion, started to falter, causing them to stumble occasionally.

Their adult children, who had grown up within the warm embrace of this home, watched with growing concern. They saw their parents' health decline, albeit gradually, and worried about their ability to age in place safely. The children cherished the memories they had created in this house, and they wanted nothing more than for their parents to continue living in the place that held so much meaning for them.

Harold, a tall and sturdy man, had always been fiercely independent. With calloused hands and a determined spirit, he took care of everything in the house. From fixing leaky faucets to cleaning the gutters, he had been the guardian of their humble abode. But lately, those once familiar tasks had become more challenging for him. He started to ignore them, hoping that somehow, they would magically fix themselves. However, his stubbornness only masked the growing concerns he had about his own abilities.

Mary, a petite woman with a twinkle in her eye, embodied a spirit of unwavering self-reliance. Throughout the years, she had poured her heart and soul into tending to their home, transforming it into a sanctuary of love and comfort. The walls radiated with the warmth of countless memories, and every corner held a piece of their shared history. For Mary, leaving the place they had called home for so long was inconceivable. It stood as a testament to the resilience and strength they had forged as a couple, and she firmly believed that they had managed just fine until now, seeing no reason to alter their way of life.

Meanwhile, their children viewed the situation from a different perspective. They couldn't help but notice the subtle signs of their parents' declining health and the challenges that their cherished home presented. They understood that both their parents and the house itself were aging and required thoughtful attention. Despite their apprehensions, the children felt compelled to broach the delicate subject of downsizing or finding a more senior-friendly residence. They were well aware that such discussions could trigger resistance and defensiveness from their beloved parents.

Navigating this emotional terrain demanded an intricate balance. The love the children held for their parents was immense, and the last thing they wanted to do was upset them. The ultimate goal was to discover a solution that would address their parents' concerns, ensuring their safety, while treading lightly to avoid unnecessary tension. With hearts full of compassion and minds grounded in understanding, the children embarked on this delicate journey, hopeful to find common ground that would be satisfying for both generations.

They called for a family meeting, gathering around the sturdy dining table that had witnessed countless family meals and conversations. They spoke about the importance of home safety as people age, emphasizing that even the most familiar and beloved houses could pose risks. They discussed the hazards that could be present in a home, from loose rugs that could cause a fall to poor lighting that could make getting around the house difficult. They shared stories of others who had adjusted their homes and the positive impact it had on their safety and well-being.

Harold and Mary listened politely, their expressions a mix of love and skepticism. They couldn't fully comprehend why they needed to change anything; after all, they had been living in the house for decades without any major incidents. To them, it was a sanctuary that had withstood the test of time.

The children, realizing that mere words might not be enough to convince their parents, decided to take a different approach. They reached out to a professional home safety assessor and arranged for an evaluation of their parents' house. On the appointed day, the family gathered as the assessor walked through each room, meticulously inspecting every corner. The assessor asked pertinent questions to encourage Harold and Mary to share any challenges they may be experiencing or things that might be harder to do, such as reach the top cabinets in the kitchen.

The assessor's findings surprised Harold and Mary. They had never realized that their beloved home could be a potential hazard. The assessor pointed out areas of concern, such as the need for a second handrail on the stairs, non-slip mats in the bathroom and better lighting in certain areas of the home. The objective evaluation brought the reality of their situation into focus, and it gave them pause for thought.

With newfound awareness, the children suggested starting with minor changes. They proposed installing the handrails and non-slip mats, making the house safer without compromising their parents' independence. Harold and Mary agreed to these initial modifications, seeing them as reasonable precautions.

However, they were still hesitant about the more significant modifications that were being proposed, such as a stairlift and an accessible bathroom. To them, these changes symbolized a reminder of their declining health, and they didn't want to feel like they were giving up their independence.

Understanding their parents' concerns, the children knew they had to be patient and empathetic. They realized that their parents were not just resisting change; they were also mourning the loss of their youth and their independence. They needed to find a way to address those concerns while ensuring their parents' safety.

One day, while the children were visiting, Harold sat down with his children and began to tell them a story. He recounted the time when he and Mary had built a fort in the backyard when their children were young. He spoke with a mixture of nostalgia and pride, recounting the joy and excitement they had all felt as a family, working together to create something special.

The children listened intently, their minds transported to a time when their parents were young and invincible. They realized that their parents valued not only the physical structure of the house but also the history and memories that were intertwined with it. It wasn't just a house; it was a vessel of their shared experiences and a symbol of their strength as a family.

This newfound understanding helped the children approach the topic one more time, but this time, they focused on finding a solution that would address their parents' concerns while still ensuring their safety. They suggested hiring a handyman to take care of the household maintenance tasks that Harold found difficult to do. This way, their parents could continue living in their home, maintaining their independence, while ensuring their safety and the increasing needs of the aging house.

# Difficult Aging in Place Conversations

To their surprise, Harold and Mary agreed to the idea. They saw it as a compromise that would allow them to stay in their home and still take care of it, without putting themselves at risk. It was a solution that honored their independence while acknowledging their changing circumstances.

As the years went by, Harold and Mary embraced the modifications to their home. They widened the bathroom door, allowing easier access, and upgraded the shower to accommodate their physical challenges. They recognized that these changes were not signs of weakness, but rather practical steps to ensure their safety and well-being.

The conversations between the generations were not always easy, but they were necessary. They required patience, understanding, and a genuine desire to find a solution that would satisfy everyone involved. In the end, Harold and Mary realized that their children were not trying to take away their independence but were simply looking out for their well-being.

Their home continued to be filled with love, laughter, and cherished memories. The walls whispered stories of the past, and the rooms still held the warmth of family gatherings. As Harold and Mary grew older, they knew deep in their hearts that they had made the right decision to address the challenges of aging in place together, as a family. Their beloved home remained a testament to their resilience, their love, and their unwavering spirit.

## Key Takeaways

While this narrative has positive family dynamics and good outcomes, realistically not every family has the same relationship. However, there are common highlights for all generations – the older, the younger and now, even another younger generation involved with family decisions. Here are some key takeaways:

## 1. Resistance to change

Harold and Mary initially resisted the idea of downsizing or making modifications to their home. They were attached to their long-standing routines and independence, which made it difficult for them to consider alternative options. This highlights the common resistance that many elderly individuals may have toward changes that are perceived as threats to their independence and autonomy.

## 2. Importance of empathy and understanding

The children recognized the need to approach the situation with empathy and understanding. They put themselves in their parents' shoes and tried to comprehend their feelings and concerns. This understanding helped them to find a more effective way to communicate and find a solution that address their parents' worries while ensuring their safety.

## 3. Home safety assessment

The professional home safety assessment played a crucial role in shifting Harold and Mary's perspective. The objective evaluation of their home hazards helped them realize that their living environment posed risks and that modifications were necessary for their safety. This emphasizes the significance of involving experts, as neutral third parties, to provide tangible evidence to support the need for change.

## 4. Finding a compromise

The children found a compromise that allowed Harold and Mary to maintain their independence while ensuring their safety. By suggesting hiring a handyman to assist with household tasks, they addressed Harold's inability to handle maintenance duties. This compromise satisfied the parents' desire to stay in their beloved home and take care of it, while also meeting their increasing needs. It highlights the importance of finding solutions that respect the wishes and values of aging individuals while addressing their safety concerns. Harold and Mary were also willing to compromise to accommodate the necessary home modification changes as they evolved. Mutual respect is enhanced as the family sees everyone participating in the solution.

Yes, getting started with these difficult conversations can be daunting. For additional guidance or suggestions for you or your family members, please reach out to Fritzi through the contact form on her website, www.householdguardians.com, and she will respond directly. You can also reach her through fritzi@agesafeamerica.com. She is delighted to share ideas from her professional and personal perspectives!

## Fritzi Gros-Daillon

AS A MASTER INSTRUCTOR for CAPS and Universal Design for NAHB and Director of Education for Age Safe America, Fritzi's mission of education for professionals on aging in place and home safety is more important today than ever. Speaking nationally, regionally, and locally and the author of the national award-winning book, "Grace and Grit: Insights to the Real Life Challenges of Aging for Adult Children and their Parents", she shares strategic, implementable solutions for successful aging in place to her audiences.

    Fritzi Gros-Daillon, MS, CSA, CAPS, UDCP, SHSS
    NAHB 2019 Educator of the Year
    CEO, Household Guardians
    Director of Education, Age Safe America

    https://linktr.ee/fritzigrosdaillon

LinkedIn
    https://www.linkedin.com/in/fritzigrosdaillon/

# Home Safety Tips

## By Pam Santoro

**Question:**

My parents are getting older and there are many things that I would like to know. For example, how can I make their home safer for them to navigate? What can I do about social isolation to help them stay connected with family and friends? And where should I go if I suspect any kind of elder abuse?

**Answer:**

What is really sad is that most 911 operators get calls of physical abuse to the elderly which are referred to the police department immediately. Some calls are just welfare checks from neighbors who usually call the local police or fire department to do a welfare check. In the North Atlanta area, the local fire departments adopted a community paramedicine service similar to what Grady Hospital has in their area. The local city fire departments are the main contact in our area for welfare check because you never know when someone has fallen in their home.

**Here are some of my home safety tips:**

- Tuck electrical and phone cords safely out of walkways.
- Ensure rugs, runners, and mats are secured.
- Test smoke detector and replace batteries.

## Difficult Aging in Place Conversations

- Install handrails throughout the home.
- Ensure porches and stairwells are well lit.
- Clear stairs, landings, and floors of clutter.
- Write and regularly review emergency plans including doctor's contact information, prescriptions, power of attorney, health directive, and your emergency contact info.

A lot of times when I meet with a senior, I walk through their home and make a safety check list. Everything I do to stage a house for sale pretty much makes it senior safe.

**Address social isolation and ways to re-engage with friends/family/community.**

Many individuals live alone away from loved ones. Take advantage of local senior center activities, community events or just attending their local church, synagogue, or mosque. You can also set up a video call with a friend or family member who will brighten up their spirits. There are also services to call and check on individuals weekly that will keep individuals socially engaged. Happy Talks is one of them. Another available service, Naborforce, hires a neighbor to drive your loved one to lunch, the grocery store, or other appointments. Dementia Spotlight, Parkinson's and Alzheimer's groups are wonderful for caregivers and seniors to find compassion and support. What I've seen with seniors who are called on weekly or taken to lunch on a regular basis is a much happier outlook. My own mom and aunts visit their senior center daily (Monday through Friday) to eat lunch, play Bingo, do chair stretches, take day trips, and play cards. Socialization is fantastic, and it keeps them going.

One of my clients lost his lovely wife two years before I met him. He was getting really lonely and wanted to move to senior living. Another real estate company wanted him to sign a contract to purchase his home. However, there was an unexplained $10,000 charge. He knew he shouldn't sign this contract and contacted the senior living community sales staff which recommended that he call me. I helped him get his wife's will to probate court by recommending an eldercare attorney. Peace of Mind Transitions packed his wife's collections and sent them to family members, then the house was staged, photographed, marketed, and sold. When I stop by Village Park Alpharetta, I still make sure to visit him. He is so happy now.

My friend and local fireman, David Allen, is a part of my Senior Resource Alliance of North Atlanta (SRANA) group. He was thrilled to meet us because there was one gentleman who called the Alpharetta Fire Department 115 times in one year. This gentleman's family lived out of state. By meeting the professionals in SRANA, David helped this gentleman get a free lift from Friends of Disabled Adults and Children (FODAC), a home care company. They visited weekly to help him. Meals on Wheels were delivered, and a cleaning service was hired. They even connected him to physicians who make house calls. His calls to the Alpharetta Fire Department decreased to 15 calls in a year instead of 115 due to connections and networking. The SRANA group has mobile physicians, dentists, audiologists, home care nurses, hospice workers, cardiologists, rehabilitation therapists, occupational therapists, mobile lab services, cleaning services, eldercare attorneys, financial advisors, reverse mortgage advisors, realtors, and more.

David Allen, My Watch Alpharetta, shared some statistics about 911 calls:

a. Non-Emergency 911 Calls Cost $169 per call (a fire truck with a crew goes out).
b. Three years of lift assists at senior living communities costs $117,000.

## Difficult Aging in Place Conversations

    c.  There are about 52 lift assists in one month which causes 911 delays. In other words, the lift assists may take help away from a true emergency like a stroke, heart attack, or fire.

**How to have a conversation about whether they should stay in their home.**

Another question David Allen asked was, "What can I say or do to help a senior that really should not be living in their home anymore? He is not bathing or caring for himself, his home is not being maintained and needs cleaning. Tell me what to say."

    My suggestion was to begin by explaining that touring a senior living community is free. The communities welcome everyone. By visiting a community, the senior can talk to residents who live there and ask about activities, dining, and costs. The social aspects of senior living will brighten their day. There are many communities who will permit you to do a 60-day trial period to test if you like it. By using this option, you still own your house if you'd like to return.

    I also encouraged him to explain that if the person does move to senior living, we could then help them with vendors and contractors to put their house in marketable condition to enable them to pay for the new senior living community easily. Having a comparable market analysis of your property is also complimentary. When someone knows the value of their home, they can make good financial decisions.

    I explained to David that if they are concerned about leaving their stuff, there are great vendors who can help them choose what to bring to their new living space, help them pack and set it up in their new space. Precious treasures can be given to family and friends. By taking a picture of the treasures, we can put their special memories in a digital photo frame so they will still be able to see their treasures and enjoy their memories.

If they would still prefer to stay in their home, we can recommend contractors to retro-fit their home to make sure that living there is safe. Contractors can add grab bars, install ramps, and stairlifts, if needed. Home care agencies could come in a few times a week to assure that they are okay. Setting them up for Meals on Wheels during the week will ensure they have a good balanced meal five times a week. House cleaning services can be set up on a weekly basis. Landscapers can be hired to do the yardwork including cleaning their gutters.

In other words, there are many options to offer someone who is not quite sure they are ready to move.

**What to do if you suspect elder abuse:**

As a local realtor in the senior industry, along with organizing the Senior Resource Alliance of North Atlanta professional group, I received this call from a child regarding the minister of her Mom's church: "What should I do if my mom's minister is holding church meetings at my mother's home, money is missing from her accounts, and other items are missing? I feel she is being taken advantage of."

The first thing to do is to immediately contact the local police department regarding elder abuse. There is normally a local division and a state division for elder care fraud.

You should also contact an elder care attorney in your area to discuss this problem. They will be able to advise you on the next steps to take.

If you are on your loved one's bank account, call the bank immediately or visit them in person. Explain what is happening and let them give you advice on how to proceed so you can protect her money.

It is also important to talk to your loved one. In this case, the daughter could explain that the minister may be taking advantage of her. Ask her to let you know when the minister will come to her home and make sure you are there.

**Be aware of quit claim deed scams.**

Another thing to be concerned about is someone taking advantage of a senior by slipping a quit claim deed amongst papers that they are signing. A lot of seniors are very trusting and can miss this extra page when signing a contract for repairs around the house. Scam artists are hurting the elderly like this. Once a quit claim deed is signed ownership transfers.

My recommendation is to add your children, or another loved one that you trust, to your deed or hire an eldercare attorney to put your property and assets into a trust.

There are many ways that you can protect your loved ones and help them stay safe in their older years. These are just a few of the examples that I have seen, but if you have any other questions, please reach out to us at the Senior Resource Alliance Network of Atlanta.

**Senior Resource Alliance of North Atlanta links:**

https://www.facebook.com/groups/240751503086441
https://www.linkedin.com/groups/12057638/

## Pam Santoro

AS A 55+ REALTY advisor specialist, I love helping seniors retro-fit their homes to live in them longer or getting a great value to be able to right-size to their next home.

Specializing in luxury real estate, relocation, resale, and new construction, Pam Santoro has experience in both the selling and buying sides of a real estate transaction. Living in the North Atlanta area for over 29 years, Pam knows the communities and neighborhoods. With over 18 years in the Atlanta Real Estate market, she is both an expert and a professional. Her computer science/business background combined with being a seasoned negotiator enables her to get the best deals for her clients.

My clients are both local and relocating to the North Atlanta area.

Contact me today to find out more!

Accredited Relocation Specialist, Luxury Marketing Specialist, 55+ Realty Advisor, Downsizing/Rightsizing Specialist

Short Sale and Foreclosure Specialist

Luxury Certified

55+ Realty Advisor Specialist

2023, 2022, 2021 & 2020 Five Star Award

2021 & 2019 Family Life Publications North Fulton Best Realtor

2015 Berkshire Hathaway HomeServices Honor Society

2018 & 2014 Ambassador of the Year – Greater North Fulton Chamber of Commerce

2011-2012 President, ABWA Crabapple Chapter

2011 American Business Women's Association Crabapple Chapter Woman of the Year

2010 Member of the Year, Atlanta Chapter, Woman's Council of REALTORS®

www.pamsantoro.bhhsgeorgia.com

www.pamsantoro.com

https://www.linkedin.com/in/pamsantoro/

https://www.facebook.com/PamSantoroRealEstate

https://goo.gl/maps/62om1ZfBMYUrgqhz7

https://www.instagram.com/pam.santoro/

https://www.youtube.com/pamsantoro

https://twitter.com/pamsantoro

https://www.tiktok.com/pamsantoro

Senior Resource Alliance of North Atlanta links:
  https://www.facebook.com/groups/240751503086441
  https://www.linkedin.com/groups/12057638/

"REALTOR® Pam Santoro is your trusted local resource in the Atlanta real estate market. After all, no one sells a home like a mom!"
  pam.santoro@BHHSgeorgia.com
  www.pamsantoro.BHHSgeorgia.com

# Some Dynamics of Home Accessibility Decisions

By Louis Tenenbaum

**Question:**

What needs to be considered when you are remodeling a home for accessibility?

**Answer:**

I have been a remodeling contractor for a very long time and focused on accessibility for more than 30 years. I have been through many homes. After all these years scoping the layouts, understanding mobility challenges, and being versed in what design and products may apply, I often have a pretty good idea what will work before introductions are complete at a first meeting. So, for me, knowing what to do is not usually the hard part. The hard parts, the difficult conversations, are about the personalities, feelings, and decisions through which I must travel with my clients.

There are a lot of similarities in our homes. That is especially true in bathrooms because the five-foot tub with three-sided surround is such a standard element. I have even worked on the same house model quite a few times. This particular design, constructed in subdivisions throughout suburbs in the Washington, DC area by a national builder, lends itself to accessibility modifications, so it is sought by buyers with mobility issues.

Still, it is not as easy as it may sound because, even in these cases where the house is the same and the solution uses tried and true details, no two projects are the same. One cannot minimize the personal nature of this work or the aesthetic sense that must be respected.

Because the market for aging in place remodeling has been slow growing, many of my projects have been households who are not questioning their capabilities or prognosis. These include families of children with disabilities, adults who have had mobility challenges their whole lives, or those for whom injury or illness brings disability early in adulthood. They called because they want to solve a problem. They are often unfamiliar with the range of solutions, the design and decision process, or costs. That is where our conversations begin. They called because they know they have a problem. My task is to help them find a functional, affordable, and attractive solution.

A key to solving the puzzle is often tied up in the budget. I don't remember a client for whom money is no object. Even if finances are not a big concern, decisions are still hard. First, problems must be identified. Can they be solved? Do they need to be solved? Are there multiple strategies to consider? What is the range of costs? How quickly can they be implemented? Who can do the work? As with the purchase of a car, home, or even vacation plans, education, re-thinking, hand wringing, and heartache is often involved in making decisions. Sometimes, since the solution is so clear to me so quickly, handling personal relations and patience are the most important tools in my kit.

Knowing the possible fixes in the first few minutes of an interview is even less significant when the call is prompted by aging. Older clients, couples, and families have many facets. There is much more that is the same in houses than in the lives of these individuals and relationships. Often there is not even agreement on whether there is a problem, let alone that it needs to be tackled, or what course of action to pursue.

## Some Dynamics of Home Accessibility Decisions

Mobility problems often come on slowly. The stiffness of arthritis, for example, may cause gait, reach, and maneuvering changes to emerge over time. There is a real possibility they are taken in stride, like tattered wallpaper, until they become problems. Out of this we learn that our ability to *not* see what is right before us is uncanny. Admirable, really, if it were not so troublesome in terms of encouraging people to prepare their homes for what may (may not) be coming, or heartbreaking when it leads to a forced move.

In one home I remember clearly, the husband showed me around on such shaky legs I was worried I would have to catch him coming down the stairs. His wife, watching this scary maneuver for the umpteenth time says, "Well, if he ever needed a wheelchair, he would just have to move out." She was not being callous. Many people associate the need for a wheelchair with substantial cognitive decline, such that clear mindedness shrouds mobility problems from being witnessed. His presence in their relationship blinded her to his physical condition. I think he already knew he sometimes needed a wheelchair. But, with her pronouncement, he was afraid to be direct in voicing his need, fearing she might just kick him to the assisted living "curb." Getting them to anything like the same page for modifying the home was just too difficult.

My read of this story is not to say the problem is denial. Our natural tendency is to foresee things going pretty well. We figure it will all work out. Most things have worked out up to now, right? Instead of denial, let's call it "rosy thinking based in experience." The wisdom we recognize as a natural and wonderful benefit of aging tells us to look at our experience as a guide. But none of us have experience in our own aging process. It is really hard to picture ourselves older, in poor health, or living with disability. We have never been there before. Additionally, longevity is brand new to the species. Neither our lived experience nor our collective consciousness includes the slow decline in capabilities that accompany aging. Rosy thinking applies to individuals, couples, and families. These factors make pro-active aging in place accessibility remodeling a tough sell.

The calls that quite typically start rolling in just before Thanksgiving are instructive because the complexity of the circumstances is compressed. A family member who is coming to town wants to meet to discuss things we can do to make mom's home safer (dad, Aunt Betty, brother Joe… fill in the blank). There is some urgency, often just what you look for in a sales meeting, right?

But the urgency is a little murky. The visitor wants to get some decisions made, maybe even a proposal signed, while they are in town. And time is further limited. There are other events, museum trips, a hike, other friends and relatives to visit, a movie, play, or concert all plan to attend. So timing is tight and tricky. The whole weekend is not available. They want a quick meeting so decisions can be made between other family events. Unfortunately, the situation is complex. The sale is not so easy.

*What is the motivation?* There is no doubt of the safety concerns. "Mom" is older. This visitor hears reports of her growing frailty, need for assistance… and maybe even the complaints from those who live in the area and provide more frequent, daily, or live-in care. Maybe the visitor wants to reduce the chance of being called in an emergency. Simple home safety upgrades seem like a great purchase to avoid that possibility. On the other hand, does the local caregiver want help or just an ear on which to vent their exhaustion and frustration? Do they want to preserve mom's money for the estate, especially since they are earning less due to the time they devote to caregiving, even if they feel really good about doing it?

*Who is making the decisions?* I always request that *all* decision makers are on deck for the initial meeting. This decision-making body may be more than one child, a spouse, sibling, and grandchildren. Perspective and rationale are established in that first conversation. If someone critical is missing at the starting point the path to decisions becomes uneven. There is also the possibility that someone has actual or tacit veto power. For example, a wealthy but more distant relative or friend from whom the family expects financial support, may have an undefined, unspoken, but outsized voice. They may not be present. The fact that someone misses the meeting because they were not invited, not informed in time, or not there for the weekend, may seed a grumpiness precluding their consent. Support and defensiveness for and against the plan emerge right away. Moving forward is difficult if everyone is not on the same page. I have never seen a project move forward when a critical decision-maker is not present at the initial meeting.

Even if everyone is there, it is really hard to know the dynamics of the assorted interests. Everyone is in a different place. Feelings are involved, even though they may not be expressed. In fact, feelings may become a huge barrier especially because they are not expressed. And very likely at least some of the parties are not even in touch with their own complex feelings. There is probably lots of history and varied circumstances in and amongst these caring individuals. As in every situation with family dynamics, what is said may be much different than what is not said.

*How does the target of all this love feel about it?* Respect must be paid to the person for whom the work and decisions are being considered. Do they recognize the concerns as legitimate? Is all this "concern" seen as "people mixing their nose in my business?" Am I being ganged up on, sowing discontent among my kids, or burdening them in ways I want to avoid? At the very least this aspect of the conversation may require some careful positioning and discussion of the needs, value, and effort being proposed.

Difficult conversations are often needed to tease out a shared understanding of the circumstances behind a call for accessibility modifications. Family dynamics often play a huge role in any decisions that are made. Unknown prognoses, timeframes, and finances must be figured into any course of action. This 'sales call' may verge on multi-party group counseling.

Sometimes a joint, comfortable, educated decision to move is the best outcome. If I can see that as a successful use of my experience, it is pretty clear knowing what remodeling to do is not the hard part, or the most important skill needed for this work.

## Louis Tenenbaum

LOUIS TENENBAUM IS a recognized authority for aging in place. A speaker, consultant and advocate, he brings together consumers, businesses, nonprofits, and policy stakeholders to drive policy and investments to increase the nation's aging in place capacity. Louis is dedicated to improving the safety, accessibility, comfort, affordability, and security of housing for an expanding senior population with increased longevity. Uniquely straddling the building, aging, and policy worlds, in 2016 Louis was named a Next Avenue "Influencer in Aging."

In the early 1990s Louis was one of the first contractors to focus his remodeling business on home safety, accessibility, and aging in place. In the late 1990s Louis participated in the National Endowment for the Arts (NEA), universal brainstorm with AARP and the National Association of Home Builders (NAHB) to lay the foundation for the Certified Aging in Place Specialist (CAPS) program. Louis served as a subject matter expert and one of the first instructors for the CAPS course.

Louis has been the home modifications expert in three startup retail ventures, the 1995 "American Health Superstore" in Rockville, MD, the 1997 Centex Home Builders "Life Solutions Store" in Falls Church, VA and Skokie, IL, and the 2008 Home Preferred concept that won first place in the Silicon Valley Boomer Venture Summit $10,000 business plan competition.

Curious why, if home modifications are such a good idea, no one does it, in 2010 Louis wrote the visionary white paper, Aging in Place 2.0: Rethinking Solutions to the Home Care Challenge published by the MetLife Mature Market Institute, describing the coordinated systems and services necessary for aging in place successfully.

Louis was a key advocate for the Design for Life tax credit program adopted in Montgomery County, MD in 2014.

In 2015 Louis Tenenbaum and Susan Kimmel co-founded the HomesRenewed™ Resource Center for research and education promoting home modifications and aging in place, publishing Summary of Consumer Interviews survey regarding home modifications motivators and tax incentive in 2016 and Making It Safe to Age in Place, presented at the Gerontology Society of America Conference in 2022.

Louis and Susan co-founded the HomesRenewed™ Coalition for political advocacy for home modifications tax incentives which, in 2022, led the introduction of HR-7676, the Home Modifications for Accessibility Act, aiming to provide incentives to homeowners who make safety updates to their homes. That movement continues in the advocacy committee of the National Aging in Place Council.

# HEALTHCARE

# Addressing Urinary Incontinence

By Colleen Bather

**Question:**

My mom is experiencing incontinence and frequent leakage. Is there anything she can do to help prevent it?

**Answer:**

Urinary Incontinence is a major risk factor for nursing home admission. This Pelvic Floor issue can happen to women or men and in this chapter, I will share some types of therapy that can help with these issues.

Did you know that approximately 32% of American women suffer from some sort of Pelvic Floor Dysfunction (PFD)?[2] But did you also know that approximately 16% of men suffer from some type of PFD as well? The prevalence of PFD is higher in women, but it is also a common problem with men. As we age, the percentage of both men and women having one or more PFDs increases as well. One of the main risk factors to being admitted to a nursing home is urinary incontinence or leakage of urine. So, trying to gain control and work on these muscles is important for prevention. There is specialized therapy for these problems which is called Pelvic Floor Physical Therapy (PFPT). And like Physical Therapy (PT), where the therapist works with your muscles, bones, and joints in places such as your shoulder, back, hips, and knees, a Pelvic Floor PT works with these structures that sit in your pelvis.

---

2   https://www.nature.com/articles/s41598-022-13501-w

## Difficult Aging in Place Conversations

The Pelvic Floor is a group of small muscles that sit like a hammock at the base of your pelvis. These muscles play a key role in your body's function. One such role is to support your pelvic organs which in women, includes the uterus, bladder, and rectum, and in men, the bladder, prostate, and rectum. Besides supporting your pelvic organs, the pelvic floor muscles aid in control and coordination of your bladder and bowel, support sexual health and assist in core strength/stabilization. If the muscles aren't working correctly, then people can suffer from one or several dysfunctions or, in other words, symptoms. So, while this is a fairly common area to have problems or issues, it's not one that people feel comfortable talking about or even sharing with friends, family, or health care workers. I see this a lot with patients hesitating or putting off going to this type of therapy out of embarrassment or not really knowing what to expect when they do go for their appointment. I find that talking and educating patients prior to coming in can help ease some of their anxiety and take some of the fear away before they enter the clinic. I'm hoping by discussing it with you today, I can answer some questions and educate you on PFPT, and also, hopefully, ease some of your fears and give you the boost or push you need to seek out this care if you need it.

One patient who comes to mind is Charlotte. She suffered for several years in silence with her symptoms of pelvic floor dysfunction. Like many people, Charlotte didn't even know that there is a specialized physical therapy to help her until a friend of hers told her about the therapy she was receiving. It took some prompting from her friend, but she finally felt comfortable enough to set up a phone consultation with me before committing to scheduling an in-person appointment. During that conversation, with some gentle prodding with questions, she felt comfortable enough to share some of her symptoms with me and open up about how these symptoms were affecting her life on a daily basis. She was having bladder leaks multiple times per day, some when she

## Addressing Urinary Incontinence

was working out at the gym as well as when she was sneezing, coughing, and laughing. By educating her on where her pelvic floor muscles are in her body and their job, she felt comfortable enough to schedule her first appointment. Taking the first step is hard sometimes, especially with this type of dysfunction. I know firsthand what it is like to be on that table because during all my training, I had to be the patient for the other Physical Therapist to learn from and vice versa. I know it's not easy to take that step to decide to have this type of therapy or to be open to talk about the symptoms you are having. But just like Charlotte, hopefully you, too, will be empowered to seek out help.

One such pelvic floor dysfunction is urinary incontinence, which is loss of control in your bladder resulting in leakage of urine. This can present itself as Stress Incontinence which are leaks related to a physical or stress activity. For example, leaks that occur while sneezing, coughing, or laughing like Charlotte was experiencing. I say to my patients when explaining this, "Did you ever see a group of women together laughing and the majority of them are crossing their legs and leaning over as they do so? This is because some of them are leaking, and they are trying to use their leg muscles to help them not leak." Other physical activities like running, jumping, walking fast, or squatting can put pressure on the bladder, and if these muscles aren't strong and/or flexible enough, it can cause bladder leaks. Urinary incontinence can also be caused by urge incontinence where someone has a strong sense of urgency to urinate and has leaks getting to the bathroom. I have several patients who complain that as soon as they pull in the driveway, it's like their bladder revs up and goes from 0 to 60, and they have to practically run family members over getting from the car to the bathroom. Some people can suffer from both forms of incontinence which is called mixed incontinence. Frequency of urination, where people feel like they are going every 30 minutes to an hour to the bathroom to void, can be present as well and again, not a fun side effect.

Another Pelvic Floor Dysfunction is fecal incontinence which is loss of bowel control resulting in fecal accidents. This can be related to urgency and/or frequency of bowel movements. While fecal incontinence can be the result of weak or tight muscles in your pelvic floor, it can be a side effect from having other gastrointestinal conditions such as Crohn's, Celiac disease, or irritable bowel syndrome (IBS). Constipation or chronic diarrhea can be problems due to your pelvic floor not coordinating properly, meaning some people don't know how to use or call on these muscles properly. Did you know that people can actually be having a bowel movement the wrong way? As a child, when we are potty training, parents just place the child up there and hope we all just figure out what to do naturally, but sometimes instead of keeping these muscles relaxed, we tighten them and close off that opening leading to things like constipation or outlet problems. Little fixes like educating someone on how to have a bowel movement correctly and what these muscles should be doing can make a huge difference in preventing several problems.

Pelvic Organ Prolapse (POP) is a dysfunction that occurs when one or more of your organs that sit in your pelvis drop, tilt, or descend from their original place in the body. In women, this can be when the bladder and/or uterus drop into the vaginal canal and can be severe enough to protrude out of the vaginal opening. During pregnancy, the pressure of the weight of the baby sitting in your pelvis and abdomen, or force of delivery, can cause the ligaments that support these organs to lose some of their integrity resulting in dropping of these organs. Charlotte had several children, and this caused her bladder to drop resulting in bladder leaks after the birth of her 3$^{rd}$ child. It got progressively worse after her 4$^{th}$ pregnancy/delivery. Over the years, her bladder prolapse worsened and caused her to leak more frequently and increase the amount she was leaking as well. Her symptoms gradually got worse and worse as her prolapse worsened. POP can cause pelvic pain, urinary incontinence, difficulty emptying the bladder or problems with having bowel movements. Men and women can both have prolapse of their rectum which can result in the difficulties mentioned above.

The role of the pelvic floor muscles in sexual health can cause issues for men and women. If the pelvic floor muscles are tight or in other words, inflexible, this can cause painful intercourse or dysfunction with normal sexual activities. Tight muscles can be tender to touch or have trigger points or spasms resulting in pain or irritation. Scars from tears or episiotomies from childbirth can also cause pain, even years after these events. After menopause, with the drop in estrogen levels, the skin that surrounds these areas can become thin, irritable, and painful to touch. Charlotte was also having some tenderness with intercourse that started after menopause but never felt comfortable discussing with her Ob-Gyn or other healthcare professional until she started Pelvic Floor PT. With some gentle stretching we did in the clinic, and working with her Ob-Gyn on hormone imbalances, she was able to have pain-free intercourse.

Pelvic pain can be a difficult symptom for people to deal with and can occur for many reasons such as: pelvic organ prolapse, tightness in the muscles, post-surgical pain like prostate cancer surgery or hysterectomy, scar tissue, coccyx/tailbone problems, or issues that stem from your hip, pelvis, or back. The nerves that sit in this hammock of muscles in the pelvis can also be compressed or pinched which can cause pain.

We covered some of the possible dysfunctions of the pelvic floor muscles, let's discuss what PFPT is and what type of treatments are used in this type of therapy. Generally, patients are seen once a week for 6-18 total visits depending on what specifically is going on with these muscles. At the first visit, an evaluation is performed by the Pelvic Floor Physical Therapist, and they will ask you several questions to get a good history of what exactly is going on with these muscles. Some questions I discussed with Charlotte were the following: "How often do you urinate?", "Do you have any pain in that area, pain with sitting, pain with intercourse, pain with urination or with a bowel movement?", "Do you always feel like you are running to the bathroom or is it difficult to make it in time to the bathroom?" During the evaluation, the PT will educate you on where the pelvic floor muscles are and what their jobs are in your body. Topics of education that may be covered are how to have a proper bowel movement (as we discussed earlier, it isn't always something we naturally know how to do correctly), what a normal day should look like regarding how often you urinate, and tips to help with frequency and controlling urgency. Education on strategies for protecting further prolapse are talked about and in Charlotte's case would have greatly benefited her from her bladder prolapse getting worse if she was taught this in her 20s or 30s.

After a thorough history is taken by the PT, an internal and external muscle evaluation is performed. By assessing these tissues, determination of flexibility of these muscles can be discerned. Sometimes weakness isn't the only issue with these muscles but rather, there can be problems with muscles being tight or inflexible which can lead to symptoms. So, the PT is looking for the tone, flexibility of these muscles as well as the strength, endurance, and coordination of these pelvic floor muscles. Surrounding areas of the pelvis are evaluated like your hips, back, abdominals, and legs. Once the evaluation is complete, then a treatment plan can be established.

Problems with weakness in the pelvic floor are addressed with a strengthening program like Kegels (a term for contracting and relaxing these muscles). Most people doing Kegels are contracting or relaxing them incorrectly, so the PT will coach and educate you on how to do this properly so that you can start gaining strength and control. Charlotte thought she was performing a Kegel the right way, but she was actually bearing down or dropping her pelvic floor rather than contracting them. With manual cueing to these muscles and using biofeedback, she was able to start to contract them the right way. Biofeedback is just a tool the PT can use to help you learn how to do Kegels properly where your contraction of these muscles is displayed on a computer screen. It's a great way to see how you are contracting these muscles and measure the strength of your contraction which can be recorded for progress. Exercises for strengthening your hips, back, and stomach can be given to help assist your pelvic floor muscles.

When treating painful or tight muscles, the focus is on relaxing and gently stretching these tissues so they are flexible and pain-free. Self-digital stretching or dilator stretching of these muscles can be taught for a home exercise program, in addition to internal and external releases done by the PT in the clinic. For people who have tight and/or painful pelvic floor muscles, Kegels are not the best approach and can make these muscles tighter and possibly more painful. Stretching exercises for the back, stomach, hips, and legs are usually given to patients for a home exercise program.

We live in a very stressful environment, and I find lots of people keep tension in their body, like clenching their jaw or holding tension in their shoulders, but did you know that the pelvic floor is another area where we grip and hold tension? Helping patients be aware that they are doing this and learning to relax those muscles, can sometimes provide more control over your bladder leaks. Because you aren't always fatiguing these muscles, they can work better.

These are a few of the treatment options for PFD but there can be several other treatments to assist in improving the function of the pelvic floor muscles. I wanted to make sure you have some of the basics down, some of your questions answered and have some resources on how to seek out care. Hopefully you feel more knowledgeable about these symptoms and what Pelvic Floor PT is so that if you are suffering in silence, as Charlotte did for years, you know there is help. Symptoms of pelvic floor dysfunction can get worse over time, so starting this type of specialized physical therapy can be beneficial to increasing your quality of life. Remember, it's never too late to start working on these muscles to gain control. I always say to my clients, "I know that no one wants to come see me. I get that, but it's really not as bad as you think once you start." As most of my patients say at the end of that first visit, "I wish I would have done this years ago." I hope you feel empowered to take control of these issues and improve your quality of life as Charlotte did.

## Colleen Bather, MPT, CCCE
Owner, Pelvic Align PT

COLLEEN BATHER has over 26 years of experience with Ortho-pedic/Sports Medicine Physical Therapy with 13 years specializing in PFPT. She graduated with her Masters of PT from Duquesne University in 1997. She then received her CCCE from Cleveland State University and coordinated student clinical rotations for over 10 outpatient sites. Colleen has received advanced training in PFPT for Women and Men including pregnancy and postpartum care, complex pelvic pain conditions, post-surgical pain, bladder dysfunctions, GI conditions, pelvic organ prolapse/repair, and post cancer care. She is the owner of Pelvic Align PT focusing on PFPT.

pelvicalignpt@gmail.com
https://www.linkedin.com/in/colleen-bather-464924229/
https://www.instagram.com/pelvicalignpt/
https://www.pelvicalignpt.com/

## Difficult Aging in Place Conversations

# Navigating a Life Changing Diagnosis
## By Tricia Bell

**Question:**

My parent was just diagnosed with a life changing diagnosis. How do I navigate this situation in a way that is supportive and proactive?

**Answer:**

I want to help you navigate through understanding and helping someone who has been diagnosed with a life ending/changing diagnosis.

I have Multiple Sclerosis (MS) and was diagnosed in June of 1999. I had some form of mobility until 7 years ago, we are in the year 2023, so I'll let you do the math depending on when you are reading this. I am getting some standing now and a bit more movement, but everyday decisions determine an outcome. Do I take a new medication or not? Should I stop taking a prescription? Do I work out today or let my body rest? Everything from eating to exercise to whether the weather is hot or cold determines my results of the day. This is true for any diagnosis, no matter what it is.

Anyone diagnosed with something faces the fact that every decision from diet to activity to exercise makes a big factor in their day. I have exercise in my weekly routine which is important especially because I am in a powerchair, not a manual, which means I'm not getting cardio. I love being out doing something rather than staying home. It makes me feel good, but I then feel guilty because I didn't do anything to exercise. I have a lot of battles every day with myself.

**How does it feel to get a terminal diagnosis?**

I consider any diagnosis to be terminal because it permanently changes us. "It" may not kill us directly, but pneumonia, or something similar, will. It's terrifying. Whether it is MS, Parkinson's, dementia, cancer, kidney failure or whatever, the results are the same. It changes your mental frame of mind, and how you live your life, and impacts those around you. So, let's look at that.

Read this section from the position you are in—the diagnosed or the caregiver/partner to the diagnosed. When faced with a diagnosis, it will change everyone's life. As the diagnosed, you will need to find the strength within. You may want to melt, have someone pick you up and do everything for you. On the other hand, you may take a deep breath, face it and be strong. Either way, those around you have their feelings of pain or anger, and you, the diagnosed, will have to learn to not be a part of their process.

As the diagnosed, you will be told what is best and what your loved ones feel you should do. What I mention more than once in this section is you, the diagnosed must be true to you. That means you must be ready to take responsibility for your actions whether you do what you want or take the suggestions of others. You cannot blame them for it not working, and you cannot blame others if what you choose doesn't work.

Keep this in mind when the party moves to another room and for whatever reason, you cannot move with everyone. Remember not to take it personally. It's hard. I've been left alone many times, and it's not personal, but feeling alone is hard. Talk to your caregiver/partner and ask them to stay with you so you feel a part of things. Explain how it makes you feel to be left alone. They might not have thought of it.

As the caregiver, let the diagnosed know where you are going or when you leave a room. Their memory may be getting bad, or some other circumstance may happen. Keep them informed, or if per se, they are lying down, it's nice for them to know if you're in the next room or if you went outside. That advice comes from experience.

As the caregiver, know their schedule, when to give medication, bathroom breaks, and food. Consistency is important to let them know you're there. It will lessen any fears or panic.

Keep their book, glasses, water nearby. Even if they need help reaching the item, it's knowing the item is there if they need it.

This section is for the diagnosed or the caregiver/partner:

The changes may be rapid or slow coming on. The disease, or even the treatment, can create a loss of memory, lack of feeling, uncontrolled movements, shaking, or pain. Become familiar with it by talking with others or reading up on it. No one person's experience is the exact same, but there are similarities. It also depends on how someone handles pain or another symptom.

My sister was diagnosed with Multiple Sclerosis about 10 years after I was. Our symptoms are similar, as with most patients, but how we handle them is different. We both have symptoms such as spasms or lack of circulation, but we handle them in different ways. I've tried different medications, and I don't stay on something longer than I must if I feel it isn't helping me. Believe me, some medications haven't been my friend. My sister tends to stay on her medications indefinitely, which I don't agree with. Of course, she doesn't agree with me changing things up either. How we handle our diagnosis is our own decision, and no one else's. Everyone can have their opinions, and I'm glad to hear them. But in the end, I'm responsible for me. I don't want to blame or cheer anyone else.

## Difficult Aging in Place Conversations

In late 2021, my friend of 20 some years called me from the hospital and asked me to come pick her up. She said she had taken an Uber over but didn't want to do that going home. I met her at the hospital, waiting for her as she walked out of the back in her robe and slippers with tears in her eyes. She had a type of MRI or something and she learned she has breast cancer. My dear friend was a mother of two. At the time, her oldest was 17 and the youngest was 13. She was a single parent with an ex-husband that was sometimes in the picture but wasn't going to be a supportive figure doing this. It was decided then that we were going to do this together. Every decision, every doctor's appointment, we walked through it together, making sure we tried to look at all the different options and get the answers together.

She had a double mastectomy, and at this point is doing fine. Fingers are crossed because it's been less than a year after her diagnosis, and there's always an opportunity for it to come back. We also know it is still in her body because they were unable to get it out of her lymph nodes. During all these appointments and ups and downs, we talked about the kids, the future, and what was to be. She made out her will. Knowing that her oldest daughter would be 18 was something of a relief, but her youngest was her greatest concern. Her daughter's father had left and hadn't been seen since, so she made arrangements with her friend that the girls had grown up with to take care of them if she didn't make it through. I had a list of phone numbers and schedules for any time that she couldn't do something or if anything happened. She tried to be the mom she always was and not let the girls down.

At this time, perhaps you've gone through a lot that leads up to this, thinking about the end. The diagnosis, all the treatments, feelings, and pain. Seek friends, family, even counseling in private. If you are the caregiver/partner, your thoughts need to be with the diagnosed. It's not about you. The hardest part is to separate your feelings and focus on the diagnosed. No one wants to lose someone to age or illness. Our feelings are not what matters. We have tomorrow, which is something our loved one does not have. If things have not been put in order, now is the time to find out what their wishes are or ask the diagnosed to get them written down. Finish the unfinished business. Here are a few questions to start you thinking:

- Where would you like to die – at home, in hospice, or somewhere else?
- Where do you want to be laid to rest?
- Would you want burial in a cemetery, natural burial, cremation, and what cemetery?
- Who would you like to be with you when you die?
- Is there anyone that you don't want around?
- Are there any music, prayers, or things to have around that you find comforting?

When it comes to losing someone, I've found it best to put your feelings aside. Let them spend the last of their time here with us completing anything that they want to. Checking off the bucket list is important to helping your loved one. If things have progressed past doing things, listen to their stories, their dreams, or whatever comes out. You'll cherish it forever. Some friends of mine wrote their life stories and put them into a book with pictures to give to each child. The books contained a memory and introduction to who each parent is/was, where they were born, things they did in their life, and things that were important to them.

Here are some questions to consider if you want to write something yourself:

- What was life like for you growing up?
- How did you meet your spouse or partner?

- Is there a memory that is giving you strength currently?
- What advice have you received that has made the greatest impact on your life, and who gave you the advice?

We have all heard of hospice. Don't be afraid of the word. They are there to support you. Hospice was a blessing when my parents passed. Don't feel alone. Let them support you by taking care of your loved one's hospital care so you can support your loved one emotionally.

Below is a description of hospice[3]:

- Medical care for people with an anticipated life expectancy of 6 months or less, when a cure isn't an option, and the focus shifts to symptom management and quality of life.
- An interdisciplinary team of professionals trained to address physical, psychosocial, and spiritual needs of the person; the team also supports family members and other intimate unpaid caregivers.
- Specialty care that is person-centered, stressing coordination of care, clarification of goals of care, and communication.
- Provided primarily where a person lives, whether that is a private residence, nursing home, or community living arrangement, allowing the patient to be with important objects, memories, and family.
- Care that includes periodic visits to the patient and family caregivers by hospice team members. Hospice providers are available 24 hours a day, 7 days a week to respond if patient or caregiver concerns arise.
- The only medical care that includes bereavement care, which is available during the illness and for more than a year after the death for the family/intimate network.

---

3  https://www.physicianspreferredhospicecare.com/

- A Medicare benefit to which all Medicare enrollees have a right. Hospice care also is covered by most private health insurance at varying levels, and in almost every state, by Medicaid. Read more about paying for hospice at https://hospicefoundation.org/Hospice-Care/Paying-for-Hospice-Care

**The Final Moments**

A dear friend of mine, John, that I had known since I was about 21, had a stroke in 2010. Our friendship went through marriages, divorces, children, and everything else through those years. His leg was greatly damaged, but he could still walk. His right arm became lame, and he became legally blind with limited sight. A "G" tube was inserted because he couldn't eat food anymore and lastly, he lost the ability to talk. After 18 years, in March 2023, he had a final stroke. He stayed in the hospital two weeks after being paralyzed. John was unable to move anything except some movement in his hands, his eyes, and he could move his head just a little. After his first stroke, he was moved into his mother's house where he had 24-hour care by her and a caregiver. I didn't write this to scare you but to show that a diagnosis of any kind affects our family, our friends, as well as us, the diagnosed. Whether it's the physical aspect of it, financial aspect, or the mental, any diagnosis is a reason to look at what our futures holds, and to be honest with ourselves about what we can manage.

My sister's mother-in-law, Pam, was diagnosed with breast cancer in 2022. Pam had three chemo treatments and decided she had enough. Of course, the family had their opinions but, in the end, it was her decision, her body, her pain. She lived the carefree life she knew she would because she put it out of her mind. She lived almost a year until her back started to hurt. The cancer was in her lungs, kidneys, and all throughout. She accepted her decision and laid down. They called hospice, and she left us in May of 2023, about two weeks after finding out that it had spread. Unlike Pam, others are suffering and have no answers. For those who are screaming and begging, "Please just let me die," we think we can't do anything to help them. Many don't know that there are only a few places in this world that allow someone to be assisted with their death. Physician-assisted suicide is legal in ten US states and the District of Columbia. We had Dr. Kevorkian, but many considered that murder. He wasn't doing it out of vengeance or anger he was doing it because someone wanted it or needed it. There is an organization that can assist if your situation could benefit from it—Compassion and Choices (www.compassionandchoices.org ).

There are no easy answers. Your friends and support groups will give you advice, but it may sound the same. Be honest with yourself whether you are caring for the diagnosed or you're the diagnosed. In a song by Michael Franti, one lyric has stayed with me: "Cause you never know how long you're gonna live til' ya' die." (Michael Franti Life In The City), The song "Life in the City" has other lines that make you realize how short life can be. I bet you think this is a dark song, but it's not. It's upbeat and reggae-ish. When faced with an end-of-life diagnosis, or one that brings questions and answers you aren't ready for, take a deep breath, open your mind, and answer them for yourself before someone else does.

**Resources:**

1. On the NAIPC.ORG website is a document called Act III.

2. Compassion and Choices:
www.compassionandchoices.org

3. Natural burial:
https://www.memorialplanning.com/burial-types/natural-burials

## Tricia Bell

I HAVE BEEN THE coordinator for the National Aging in Place Council for over a year. I was diagnosed with MS, confined to a wheelchair but make every effort to live a normal life and help others to do the same with their challenges. In 1997 my Mom received a diagnosis of Parkinson's. Through the years I helped my Dad care for her and learned much about the needs of finding in-home care, assisted-living, memory care, so many things. She died in 2010. After she died, and my father, declined, eventually dying of cancer, it was much easier, especially because he was very aware of what was happening and what decisions needed to be made after going through everything with my mom.

As for the personal side of me, I am an animal advocate for rescue, I have a website PetExpress.net that supports animal rescue and a blogger for it. I am a classic car enthusiast and relax doing mosaic art.

# End-of-Life Wishes

## By Ronnie Genser, Bereavement Navigators

**Question:**

Do you know what would your loved one(s) (i.e., especially a spouse or partner, or other relative, such as a brother, sister, or parent) would want should he/she suffer a major heart attack that then required life support? Or what would happen if they had a different major illness, which if they survived, would not allow them to return to the life they once had?

In addition, have you first thought about what your *own* answer to the above question would be, regarding your own medical and non-medical wishes?

If yes, have you also documented both your medical and non-medical wishes?

For your loved ones, do they have the most recent version?

**Answer:**

Smart911.com is a lifesaving service recognized by thousands of trusted sources across the country and goes through an annual SOC 2 with HIPAA/HITECH assessment to confirm all security controls are appropriate and effective. Do they have the ID & password to your records on this website?

Do your loved ones know where the master dated copies of these documents, including your Advance Directive and Physician Orders for Life-Sustaining Treatment (POLST), are located – both the electronic version and the in-print version, and are they easily accessible? Suggestions of where to locate these documents include:

a. Near where your drugs are stored
b. In a clear plastic bag hung on your refrigerator so anyone, including emergency personnel who need to enter your home, can quickly find them
c. In your wallet
d. In the glove compartment of your car, with your Advance Directive and POLST (in case you are in an accident so first responders can find them)
e. In the folder you may have for your primary care doctor.

If needed, do they have passwords to these documents, or have keys to a safe where these documents are stored, and have they been provided? Are these documents in sync, meaning does the electronic version and the in-print version include the exact same content?

Is all the information one would need to know, such as finances, passwords, etc. also documented and updated *immediately* in your documents when any information changes, and are you providing this updated document to everyone mentioned above as the documents change, so they have the most current information should you need immediate care?

Have you also shared a copy of your document with your primary care physician as well as any other physicians that provide care for any specialized medical conditions you may have? In addition, do you know that Medicare now pays for two half-hour conversations with one's primary care physician to discuss one's end-of-life medical wishes? This payment is only available when you schedule your appointment with your physician after you have satisfied your Medicare annual deductible.

Do your four major non-medical service providers (i.e., your attorney, financial advisor, accountant, insurance agent) know who your loved ones are and how to contact them?

Do your loved ones also know who your on-going non-medical service providers (i.e., housekeeper, trainer, landscaper, HVAC, etc.) are, as well as how to contact them by phone and by email should an occasion arise where they need to contact them?

So why is having this conversation so important? To possibly save your, or a loved one's, life.

When should you have this conversation? If you haven't had this conversation, then as soon as possible, because one never knows what the future holds.

Where should you have this conversation? In a quiet place where all involved are present. It can be in person or via Zoom.

How do I have this conversation with my loved ones and what are some resources to help me have this conversation? The Conversation Project (www.theconversationproject.org) whose tagline is: Helping people share their wishes for care through the end-of-life, is a great resource.

Lastly, have you also discussed your own answer to the above question with your loved one(s) and provided them with the documentation suggested above? If not, then as Ellen Goodman, founder of The Conversation Project says: "It's always too soon until it is too late…"

# Ronelle "Ronnie" Genser

SINCE 2012, BEREAVEMENT Navigators has assisted widows and widowers with the myriad of non-legal, non-financial advisory, and non-accounting/tax tasks they are faced with after the death of their loved one. Bereavement Navigators' #1 objective is to provide services to make this sometimes painful process of navigating these tasks and the journey ahead easier for them.

**Member:**

- Atlanta Senior Business Network, 2019 – present.
- Dekalb County (Georgia) Senior Provider Network, 2019 – present.
- Senior Services Partners (part of Senior Services North Fulton), 2019 – present.
- Senior Industry Networking Group, 2019 – present.
- Aging2.0 - Atlanta, 2018.
- Senior Resource Alliance of North Atlanta, 2018 – present.

- Georgia Gerontology Society, 2017 – 2018.
- Georgia POLST Collaborative (promotes POLST usage), 2017 – present. Served on: Public Policy Committee (2019); Education committee (2018).
- National Aging in Place Council – Greater Atlanta Chapter, 2016 – present. Serves on the Marketing committee.
- Atlanta Senior Care Niche Network, 2015 – present.
- Congregation Or Hadash; Member, Chesed (Kindness) Committee, 2010 – present.
- Hadassah - Life member; Member, Hadassah Greater Atlanta, Health Professionals group.
- Executive Positions and Awards:
- Advisory Council, Georgians for End-of-Life Options, 2021 – present.
- Board of Directors, Lifespan Resources, 2018 – 2023.
- Steering Committee, The Transition Network, Atlanta Chapter, 2013 – 2014.
- National Support Group Coordinator, Lewy Body Dementia Association, 2006 – 2011. Grew their support group network from 5 support groups to almost 100 support groups, spanning 36 states and the province of Ontario, Canada. Named their 2009 Volunteer of the Year.
- Board of Directors, Lewy Body Dementia Association, 2006 – 2008.
- Board of Directors and Marketing Committee Chair, Congregation Or Hadash, 2003 – 2005. Named their 2005 Woman of Achievement. Executive Committee, American-Israel Chamber of Commerce, Southeast Region, 1996 – 2007. Chaired their

Eagle Star Gala (annual fundraiser) for the first two years (2002 and 2003). Named their 1999 Woman of Achievement.
- Board of Directors, American-Israel Chamber of Commerce, Southeast Region, 1994 – 2011.
- Board of Directors, Jewish Family Services, 1991 – 1994; Chair, 102nd Annual Meeting, 1992.

# Surgery and Older Adults

By Mathius Marc Gertz, MBA, AFC®, CAPS, CDLP®

**Question:**

My parent is about to undergo surgery, and I am not sure how to prepare them? What are some of the considerations that will help me to support them through this procedure?

**Answer:**

Before I was thirty, I had had three serious accidents and several lacerations to various parts of my body. No, I was not suicidal. I was just very active and infused with a very typical youthful belief in my immortality—the kind that gets you into situations that you might otherwise avoid. After the last one, I promised myself I would try to be more prudent.

In my 50s , I had a hernia repaired. It was not that big of a deal, but I did notice a slight slowing of my step as I recovered. To be honest, I didn't pay much attention to it. Then in my sixties, I had eight surgeries in five years. I am thick-headed and completely forgot my promise to myself. The first was from an accident that caused me to be catheterized for ten months, which I wrote a book about titled, *Men and SupraPubic Catheter Survival Tips (ArminLear Press 2022)*. But after that, I had a series of elective or health-related surgeries, and by the last one, to repair a degenerative disc issue in my upper spine, my step and recovery time had significantly slowed. Short of avoiding future surgery, how could I minimize this extended recovery time?

According to an article from CNBC,[4] Recent studies and work at hospitals across the country suggest people, particularly older patients, should mentally and physically prepare to be on the operating table. "At the University of California, San Francisco's Surgery Wellness Program, older patients gear up for surgery by meeting with dieticians and physical and occupational therapists. The program will soon launch a digital app called Prehab Pal, in which algorithms prescribe older patients a plan to prepare for surgery."

"Prep is as important if not more important than the surgery itself," said Dr. Ronnie Rosenthal, chair of the American College of Surgeons Geriatric Surgery Task Force.

## Five things that pre-surgery patients can do:

### 1. Start planning early.
- Assume you may not be mobile.
- Lean on family for help.
- Stock up on food.
- Wash your laundry.
- Have a second person present when the doctor is giving information about recovery.

### 2. Take walks.
- Walking 20 minutes a day two to three weeks before surgery will shorten recovery time.
- If you have balance issues, do it at a gym or at home.

---

4 "Older Patients Recover From Surgery Faster if They 'Train' for It." www.cnbc.com, 11 Feb. 2018, www.cnbc.com/2018/02/08/older-patients-recover-from-surgery-faster-if-they-train-for-it.html.

- Get a pedometer and slowly increase your distance.

**3. Cut out your vices.**
- Experts recommend that older patients eat smaller, more frequent, and protein-rich meals beforehand.
- Stop smoking two months prior to surgery.
- Stop drinking alcohol at least two weeks prior to surgery.
- For some, giving up caffeine will help in stopping cigarettes and alcohol.
- Tell your doctor about every medication or supplement you are taking. **Don't be shy about it.**

**4. Prepare mentally.**
- Dr. Gretchen Schwarze, a vascular surgeon, and medical ethicist at the University of Wisconsin in Madison, says, the aftereffects of surgery blindside many older patients.
- You need to ask your surgeon to give you an idea of what you are in for in your recovery. "Surgery doesn't fix the problem and make you like you were before," Schwarze said. "You may be better off, but you will never be the same again."

**5. Get your finances in order.**
- Get things paid a month in advance if you can afford it.
- Make arrangements to have someone available to help you:
  i. Write checks.
  ii. Pick up your mail.
  iii. Mail your bills.
  iv. Balance your checkbook

Humans have been endowed with a fight, flight, or surrender mechanism built into our brains for survival. It is not normal for humans to voluntarily allow themselves to be knocked out and cut open. Anesthesia has made surgery an almost commonplace solution for many medical problems. But our brains haven't caught up. Allow yourself the privilege to recover slowly. Don't hurry back to your daily routine. Respect that you need your time, and don't feel guilty about it. Ask your family or friends for help, and remember, there is no shame in being good to yourself and prioritizing your recovery.

"Everything I share in my book that I mentioned earlier, I learned by trial and error. Nobody shared any of this with me—not the doctors, surgeons, nurses, or technicians. I am probably not the first man to try these solutions, but it seems I am the first to write them down for the benefit of others. Some of this stuff is embarrassing. Most of it is uncomfortable to discuss, and I suspect that most men don't. Living with a catheter, short- or long-term, changes your relationship to time."[5]

It's absolutely imperative that you SLOW DOWN. As my mother taught me, unless someone is bleeding out, bones are showing, organs have relocated, something is on fire, or someone forgot how to breathe, it's not an emergency. It will all work out. It's not a tragedy nor the end of the world.

Recovery is going to take you longer, too.

"Make time to do what you need to do. Be proactive about appointments. Leave extra time to drive somewhere. Depending upon your age and health, it will take you between 30 minutes to 1 hour more in the morning and at night to get ready for your day and to get ready for bed.

When you are older and recovering from surgery, there are many little things that you can do that will improve your recovery time. Cleanliness is one and another is to go to PT if it is prescribed. One

---

[5] Gertz, Mathius M. *Men And Suprapubic Catheter Survival Tips: How to Be Superman With Your Catheter.* 2022.

of the biggest single problems in medicine today is non-compliance. It means the patient does not trust the doctor, or at least, doesn't trust the doctor enough to push themselves to follow through with an after surgery prescription.

We have been conditioned by television commercials over the last 50 years to believe that we should have a life free and clear of pain. That is not true. Pain is part of living. After surgery, you are going to be uncomfortable and not just short term. Having PT is a necessary part of many recoveries, and it includes you also doing those exercises at home or the gym when no one is looking. You have to push yourself. It may hurt a bit. But cutting through muscles requires time and effort to rebuild them."[6]

Your routines are vital. Get into them!
- Shower at least once or twice a day.
- Empty the trash in the bathroom regularly.
- To save time in the morning, do some morning routines before you go to bed.
- Put out the things you need where you can find them.
- Set your clothes out the night before.
- Make the bed every morning.
- Get in a new habit of walking at least 20 minutes every day.

My father was one of four brothers. They were all close in age. He lived 20 years longer than any of them and died at 97 years old. Why? I believe it was because he walked a lot every day. He got his heart rate up. Got his blood flowing.

If this is not part of your normal routine, work up to it slowly, but do it. A little ache can be good for you. Remember, after 30 to 45 days of walking every day, it will become routine, and you will wonder how

---

[6] Gertz, Mathius M. *Men And Suprapubic Catheter Survival Tips: How to Be Superman With Your Catheter*. 2022.

you ever lived without it. One older adult I spoke to said that he got his walking in every morning and every evening when he walked his dog. I pointed out to him that he didn't have a dog. He smiled and said, "I used to have a dog. The dog died and I kept walking. It's a great way to socialize. You meet some of the nicest people and some very nice dogs." Works for me.

Finally, here are 10 ways to improve your recovery from surgery. Some of this we have already talked about, but here is a nice list to remember. Many of these items will be covered in your discharge papers. Make the time to read them and keep them where you can refer back to them.

1. Follow your healthcare provider's instructions.
2. Keep your follow-up appointments.
3. Prevent infection.
4. Inspect your incision for infection.
5. Care for your incision as per your release instructions.
6. Eat and drink properly.
7. Cough and sneeze carefully.
8. Know when to go to the ER.
9. Control your pain.
10. Get moving.

Remember, when the surgery is done, that is when recovery begins. And it takes longer than you think. When I was in college, I was told to figure two hours of study for every hour of classes. So, If I had 20 hours of classes a week, I needed to plan for 40 hours of study. Well, most surgery is planned about two to three months in advance. Using the college theory, figure on six to nine months of recovery time. Use this ratio and you will be able to pick up where you left off and enjoy your life after surgery.

## Mathius "Marc" Gertz

MATHIUS "MARC" GERTZ is a gifted storyteller and has been a lifelong collector of experiences. Whether good, indifferent, or bad, he has always preferred them to material gifts and enjoyed them all, one way or another. Born and raised in Brooklyn, NY, he lives with his family in Los Angeles, CA. Marc (an homage to a favored cousin) as he is known in the mortgage industry, holds an MBA and is Certified as a Divorce Lending Professional. He is a member of the Producers Guild of America, the National Reverse Mortgage Lenders Association, among others, and a published author. Marc has impeccable integrity, loyalty, honesty, empathy, and high achievement goals—the one you want on your side in any challenging life or business situation. You can learn more about him and his work at www.reverseyourthinking.mortgage

DIFFICULT AGING IN PLACE CONVERSATIONS

**LinkedIn**

https://www.linkedin.com/in/mathius-marc-gertz/

**Facebook name**

https://www.facebook.com/reverseyourthinking

**Instagram or IG**

https://www.instagram.com/rytreverse/
@rytreverse

**Business website**

https://www.reverseyourthinking.mortgage/

**YouTube channel**

https://www.youtube.com/channel/UCQS6CEfm95BNIfn-n32QKrA

# Discussing Housing, Treatment, and Care Options with a Loved One after a Difficult Diagnosis

By Gina LaPalio-Lakin

**Question:**

My friend is in a difficult situation – she's 100, recently diagnosed with stage 4 kidney disease and has outlived her assets. I'm not sure what to do or say or how I can be helpful during this time?

**Answer:**

You get the call – the call no one wants. Receiving a difficult diagnosis can be an emotionally challenging experience for both the individual and their loved ones. Alongside grappling with the diagnosis itself, discussions about housing, treatment, and care options can be equally daunting. These conversations require empathy, understanding, and careful consideration to ensure the well-being and comfort of the diagnosed individual. This chapter aims to provide guidance on how to effectively navigate these discussions, emphasizing the importance of open communication, mutual respect, planning, and the involvement of healthcare professionals. By incorporating these strategies, families and friends can foster an environment that encourages the exploration of appropriate options tailored to the specific needs of their loved one.

Whether it is you or someone you love who has received a difficult diagnosis, I hope this chapter gives you some insight on how to best plot a course down the road that may lie ahead.

## I. Establishing a Foundation of Trust and Open Communication

Building trust and fostering open communication are essential foundations when engaging in difficult conversations. By creating a safe and supportive environment, demonstrating empathy and active listening, and establishing trust and understanding, families can ensure that these conversations are productive, respectful, and centered around the well-being of the diagnosed individual.

Creating a safe and supportive environment is essential to setting the stage for effective communication. Choosing the right time and place for the conversation can make a significant difference. It is important to select a location where the diagnosed individual feels comfortable and secure, minimizing distractions, and ensuring privacy. By setting the appropriate atmosphere, loved ones can encourage openness and emotional vulnerability.

Demonstrating empathy and active listening is another vital aspect of establishing trust and open communication. It is crucial to acknowledge the emotions experienced by the diagnosed individual and their loved ones. Validating their concerns, fears, and anxieties helps them feel understood and supported. Active listening involves being fully present and attentive, offering undivided attention, and focusing on the individual's words and non-verbal cues. By actively engaging in the conversation and expressing empathy, loved ones can create an environment that encourages the diagnosed individual to share their thoughts and feelings openly.

Establishing trust and understanding is another cornerstone of effective communication during difficult discussions. Transparency and honesty are key elements in building trust. Loved ones should strive to provide accurate information and avoid withholding relevant details, as this can lead to confusion and mistrust. It is also vital to manage expectations and address potential conflicts proactively. By openly discussing concerns and potential areas of disagreement, families can work together to find common ground and maintain a supportive atmosphere.

## II. Approaching the Conversation with Sensitivity and Respect

When facing a difficult diagnosis, engaging in conversations about housing, treatment, and care options requires approaching the discussion with sensitivity and respect. It is necessary to acknowledge the individual's autonomy and preferences, present options without overwhelming them, and encourage the involvement of healthcare professionals. By fostering an atmosphere of compassion and understanding, families can navigate these challenging conversations in a manner that upholds the dignity and well-being of their loved one.

One of the fundamental aspects of approaching the conversation with sensitivity and respect is acknowledging the individual's autonomy and preferences. Recognizing that the diagnosed individual should have a say in decisions regarding their own care is crucial. It is important to respect their wishes and involve them in the decision-making process. By valuing their autonomy, families can empower the diagnosed individual and ensure that their preferences are considered throughout the decision-making journey.

Presenting options without overwhelming the individual is another central element of a sensitive and respectful approach. Breaking down information into manageable parts and providing clear explanations can help alleviate stress and confusion. Visual aids, written materials, or access to online resources can enhance understanding and make complex information more accessible. It is important to allow the individual time to process the information and ask questions, while remaining patient and supportive throughout the conversation.

## *III. Gathering Information and Educating Yourself*

Receiving a difficult diagnosis for a loved one can be overwhelming and leave family members feeling uncertain about the best course of action. In such situations, gathering information and educating oneself about the diagnosis, its implications, available treatment options, and care alternatives becomes crucial. By following these guidelines, families can make informed decisions that prioritize their loved one's well-being.

To begin, understanding the diagnosis and its implications is vital. It is essential to consult healthcare professionals and seek accurate information from reliable sources. Schedule appointments with the primary care physician or specialist to discuss the diagnosis in detail. Ask questions, seek clarification, and request written materials or resources for further reading, and consider getting a second opinion. Understanding the nature of the diagnosis, potential progression, and associated symptoms will help family members gain a clearer picture of what to expect and how to plan accordingly.

Exploring various housing options is another critical aspect of gathering information. Depending on the diagnosed individual's needs and preferences, different housing arrangements may be appropriate. Assisted living facilities, in-home care services, and community-based programs are some of the options to consider. Researching each option thoroughly, visiting facilities, and talking to professionals in the field will provide valuable insights. Understanding the level of assistance, amenities, and costs associated with each housing option will help families make well-informed decisions tailored to their loved one's specific needs.

## Discussing Housing, Treatment, and Care Options

In addition to housing options, researching treatment and care alternatives is essential. Beyond traditional medical approaches, there may be complementary therapies, alternative medicines, or clinical trials that could offer additional options for managing the diagnosis. Researching the benefits and risks of each alternative, as well as consulting with medical professionals specializing in the particular diagnosis, can provide valuable perspectives. Engaging with support groups and online communities dedicated to the specific condition can also offer insights into the experiences of others and provide information about potential treatment and care avenues. More on housing and care options in section VI.

While gathering information and educating oneself, it is important to remain critical of the sources consulted. Reliable sources may include reputable medical websites, academic journals, and information from trusted healthcare professionals. Avoid relying solely on anecdotal evidence or unverified information found on the internet, as this can lead to misinformation and confusion.

Remember, knowledge is power, and with it, families can make informed decisions to support their loved one's journey.

## *IV. Advance Directives and Planning Ahead*

Conversations about advanced directives and end-of-life wishes are difficult but necessary discussions to have with loved ones. While these topics may be uncomfortable, addressing them can provide peace of mind and ensure that an individual's preferences are respected. This section aims to provide guidance on how to approach these conversations sensitively and effectively. By emphasizing open communication, active listening, and providing information, families can engage in productive discussions that honor their loved one's wishes.

Different types of advanced directives provide individuals with the opportunity to make important decisions about their medical care in advance. Here are three common types:

1. **Living Will**: A Living Will is a legal document that outlines an individual's preferences for medical treatment in specific situations, such as end-of-life care. It typically addresses issues such as resuscitation, life support, pain management, and organ donation. A Living Will ensures that an individual's wishes regarding medical interventions are respected even if they are unable to communicate them at the time.

2. **Durable Power of Attorney for Healthcare**: This type of advanced directive designates a trusted individual, known as a healthcare proxy or agent, to make medical decisions on behalf of the person creating the document. The healthcare proxy is granted the authority to act when the individual is unable to make decisions due to incapacitation or inability to communicate. This ensures that someone trusted and familiar with the individual's values and preferences can make healthcare choices aligned with their wishes.

3. **Do-Not-Resuscitate (DNR) Order**: A DNR order instructs healthcare providers not to attempt cardiopulmonary resuscitation (CPR) in case of cardiac arrest. This directive is appropriate for individuals who do not wish to undergo aggressive life-saving measures when their heart stops. It is typically signed by a healthcare professional after thorough discussions with the individual and their family members. In some states, a DNR order is also referred to as a POLST or Practitioner Order for Life Sustaining Treatment.

It is important to consult with a healthcare professional or attorney to understand the specific legal requirements and guidelines associated with each type of advanced directive. These documents serve as valuable tools in ensuring that an individual's wishes for medical care are respected, even when they are unable to make decisions themselves.

## Five Wishes

The Five Wishes (www.fivewishes.org) document is a comprehensive tool that goes beyond traditional advanced directives to address an individual's personal, emotional, and spiritual needs. It provides a framework for expressing end-of-life wishes in a clear and organized manner.

The Five Wishes document is designed to guide end-of-life care decisions and honor an individual's values, beliefs, and personal preferences. It is often used as a complement to other advanced directives, providing a more holistic approach to end-of-life planning. The document is divided into five sections, each addressing different aspects of an individual's wishes. The different sections encompass topics such as treatment preferences, matters of dignity, communication preferences, the desire for forgiveness or reconciliation, emotional and spiritual care and preferences.

Overall, the Five Wishes document offers a beautiful approach to end-of-life planning by addressing personal, emotional, and spiritual aspects of care. It provides a structured format for individuals to communicate their preferences and allows loved ones and healthcare providers to better understand and respect their wishes. By utilizing the Five Wishes document, in addition to traditional advanced directives discussed above, individuals can have a voice in their care decisions and ensure that their values and beliefs are upheld throughout their end-of-life journey.

## *V. Developing a Comprehensive Plan*

When a loved one receives a difficult diagnosis, it is essential to develop a comprehensive plan that addresses their housing, treatment, and care needs. By engaging in collaborative decision-making, evaluating financial aspects, and creating a support network, families can ensure that their loved one receives the best possible care and support during their journey.

Evaluating financial aspects is a central element of developing a comprehensive plan. Healthcare expenses, housing costs, and ongoing care requirements can have significant financial implications. Exploring insurance coverage, government programs, and potential financial assistance options is essential to ensure that the necessary resources are available to support the diagnosed individual's needs. Researching and understanding the financial landscape can help families make informed decisions that align with their budget and ensure the availability of necessary resources.

Creating a support network is equally important when developing a comprehensive plan. Engaging with support groups, counseling services, and other community resources can provide much-needed emotional support and guidance for both the diagnosed individual and their family members. These networks offer an opportunity to connect with others who are facing similar challenges and share experiences, coping strategies, and valuable information. Reaching out to friends and extended family for assistance can also help alleviate the caregiving burden and provide additional support to the diagnosed individual.

Additionally, seeking professional guidance from healthcare providers and specialists familiar with the specific diagnosis is crucial in developing a comprehensive plan. Their expertise and knowledge can provide invaluable insights and recommendations tailored to the diagnosed individual's unique needs. Social workers, case managers, and other healthcare professionals can offer guidance on available resources, facilitate access to appropriate services, and ensure that the comprehensive plan addresses all aspects of the individual's care.

## Discussing Housing, Treatment, and Care Options

When facing a difficult diagnosis, hiring a geriatric care manager can be a valuable and beneficial decision. A geriatric care manager is a professional who specializes in coordinating and managing the care needs of older adults, including those with complex health conditions. Here are some reasons why hiring a geriatric care manager can provide a helpful aspect of developing a comprehensive plan:

1. **Expertise and Guidance**: Geriatric care managers have extensive knowledge and experience in navigating the complexities of healthcare systems, long-term care options, and community resources. They can provide expert guidance and help individuals and their families understand the available care options, make informed decisions, and develop a comprehensive care plan tailored to the specific needs and preferences of the individual. Their expertise can help alleviate the stress and confusion associated with managing the care of a loved one with a difficult diagnosis.

2. **Care Coordination**: Managing a difficult diagnosis often involves multiple healthcare providers, specialists, and support services. Geriatric care managers excel in coordinating and integrating these various aspects of care. They can streamline communication between healthcare professionals, facilitate appointments, ensure medications are properly managed, and help with care transitions, such as hospital-to-home transitions or moving to a long-term care facility. This coordinated approach ensures continuity of care and enhances the overall well-being of the individual.

3. **Advocacy and Support:** Geriatric care managers act as advocates for their clients, ensuring their rights and wishes are respected within the healthcare system. They provide emotional support to both the individual and their family, offering a compassionate and understanding presence during difficult times. Geriatric

care managers can also help with navigating insurance coverage, accessing financial assistance programs, and addressing any legal or financial concerns related to care. Their support can provide reassurance and peace of mind to the individual and their family members.

4. **Personalized Care**: Geriatric care managers take a person-centered approach to care, considering the unique needs, values, and goals of the individual. They collaborate closely with the individual and their family to understand their preferences and priorities. By taking into account factors such as personal interests, cultural background, and social support networks, geriatric care managers can ensure that the care plan is tailored to the individual's specific needs and enhances their overall quality of life.

Developing a comprehensive plan when faced with a difficult diagnosis is essential to ensure that the diagnosed individual receives the best possible housing, treatment, and care. By engaging in collaborative decision-making, evaluating financial aspects, and creating a support network, families can navigate the challenges more effectively. By taking a proactive and inclusive approach, families can provide the necessary care and support to navigate the journey of a difficult diagnosis with resilience and compassion.

## VI. *Housing and Care Options*

When a difficult diagnosis is given, exploring housing and care options becomes central to ensure the well-being and quality of life for the diagnosed individual. There are various factors to take into account, including financial considerations, the availability of caregivers, and the decision to stay at home with assistance or move to a senior housing facility.

## Discussing Housing, Treatment, and Care Options

Financial considerations play a significant role in determining housing and care options. It is essential to assess the financial resources available, including insurance coverage, savings, and potential government programs or assistance. Understanding the costs associated with different care options, such as in-home care services or senior housing, will be important to make informed decisions.

Deciding between receiving care at home with assistance or moving to a senior housing facility depends on the individual's needs, support network, and preferences. In-home care allows individuals to remain in the comfort of their own homes while receiving necessary support from professional caregivers. This option may be suitable for individuals who prefer familiar surroundings and have a strong support system of family or friends available to provide additional assistance.

On the other hand, moving to a senior housing facility, such as assisted living or nursing homes, can provide a higher level of care and support. These facilities offer a range of services, including assistance with personal care, activities of daily living, medication management, and access to healthcare professionals. They also provide social engagement opportunities and a supportive community environment. However, it is important to consider the individual's desires and the specific services and amenities offered by different senior housing options. It also bears mentioning here that not all facilities are created equal. Do your due diligence by researching each facility's state survey/inspection results and their Medicare star rating (medicare.gov), as well as touring each one you are considering.

Another aspect to consider is the availability and capacity of caregivers. In some cases, family members may take on the role of primary caregivers, providing care and support at home. This arrangement requires careful consideration of the physical, emotional, and financial impact on the family members involved. It may also be necessary to explore respite care options to provide temporary relief for family caregivers.

In instances where family caregivers are unavailable or unable to provide the necessary care, professional caregiving services become a vital part of the care team. These services can range from part-time assistance with daily tasks to full-time care, depending on the individual's needs. Hiring professional caregivers may require careful assessment of their qualifications, experience, and compatibility with the diagnosed individual's requirements.

Ultimately, the decision regarding housing and care options should be based on the diagnosed individual's unique needs, preferences, and available resources. Open communication among family members, healthcare professionals, and the diagnosed individual is essential to ensure that the chosen option aligns with their physical, emotional, and financial well-being. Taking the time to research and explore different options will help families make informed decisions that prioritize the comfort, safety, and overall quality of life for their loved one.

## *VII. End-of-Life Considerations*

Palliative care and hospice care (both billable to Medicare as of this writing) are two forms of specialized healthcare that provide support and comfort to individuals facing serious illnesses or nearing the end-of-life. These services focus on enhancing the quality of life, managing symptoms, and providing emotional and spiritual support to both the patient and their loved ones. When the time is right, palliative care and hospice care can offer invaluable support and ensure that the individual's physical, emotional, and spiritual needs are met.

Palliative care is a multidisciplinary approach that aims to improve the quality of life for individuals with serious illnesses, regardless of their prognosis. It can be provided alongside curative treatments and focuses on symptom management, pain relief, and addressing the psychosocial and spiritual needs of patients and their families. Palliative care teams consist of healthcare professionals, such as doctors, nurses, social workers, and chaplains, who work together to provide comprehensive support and guidance. This type of care can be accessed at any stage of illness and is not limited to end-of-life situations.

Hospice care, on the other hand, is specifically designed for individuals who have a terminal illness and are no longer pursuing curative treatments. Hospice care aims to provide comfort, pain management, and emotional support to patients in the final stages of their life. It is typically provided in a home-like setting, but it can also be delivered in hospitals or specialized hospice facilities. Hospice care teams work closely with patients and their families to develop personalized care plans that meet their unique needs and wishes. These plans often include pain management, assistance with activities of daily living, counseling services, and support for family members during the grieving process.

Both palliative care and hospice care prioritize the physical, emotional, and spiritual well-being of individuals and their families. They emphasize open communication, shared decision-making, and respecting the individual's wishes and goals of care.

When it's appropriate, palliative care and hospice care offer a supportive and compassionate approach to care. They provide an interdisciplinary team of healthcare professionals who work collaboratively with the individual and their loved ones to ensure that their physical, emotional, and spiritual needs are addressed. These services aim to enhance the quality of life, provide comfort, and offer support during the journey of serious illness and end-of-life.

Another aspect of end-of-life care that should be discussed, is planning ahead for one's funeral. Pre-paid funeral arrangements involve planning and paying for funeral expenses in advance. This proactive approach allows individuals to make important decisions about their funeral and relieve their loved ones from the financial and logistical burdens associated with planning a funeral during a time of grief. The ability to personalize and customize the funeral according to one's wishes, values, beliefs, and cultural or religious traditions can help minimize disagreements or conflicts among family members during an already emotionally challenging time.

In conclusion, engaging in conversations about housing, treatment, and care options after a difficult diagnosis is received can be emotionally charged and complex. However, by fostering an environment of trust, empathy, and open communication, families can navigate these discussions with greater ease and effectiveness. Gathering reliable information, considering individual preferences, and involving healthcare professionals will empower families to make informed decisions. Developing a comprehensive plan that addresses the diagnosed individual's needs, financial considerations, and support networks will ensure a holistic approach to their well-being. Remember, while these conversations may be challenging, they provide an opportunity for families to come together, provide support, and strive for the best possible outcomes for their loved one facing a difficult diagnosis. In the end, your family member or friend will undoubtedly appreciate what you have done for them.

*Some of the content contained in this chapter was written with contributions from ChatGPT. All content has been reviewed, adapted, and approved by the author, a human being.*

OpenAI. (2023). *ChatGPT* (Mar 14 version) [Large language model].

## Gina LaPalio-Lakin, M.A.

GINA HAS WORKED IN Gerontology and Geriatric services for over 30 years and holds a master's degree in Gerontological Psychology from the Adler School of Professional Psychology in Chicago. She has extensive experience in Adult Day Services, Senior Social Services, and Nursing Home Administration and served a two-year term as Coordinator for the Illinois-Missouri Gateway Geriatric Education Center at Rush University Medical Center. Gina began her tenure with Wisdom Eldercare in 2011 as a Geriatric Care Manager and has been a passionate advocate in assisting clients to access needed services, identify and achieve care goals, and enhance their overall quality of life.

When the founder and owner of Wisdom Eldercare made the decision to retire in 2019, Gina enthusiastically embraced the opportunity to acquire the company. As the new CEO/owner, Gina says the best part of her new role is that she can continue Wisdom's 35 year legacy of helping give families peace of mind, knowing their loves ones are well cared-for by reliable, compassionate caregivers at home.

# Medication Matters

By Gretchen "Gigi" Marquardt

**Question:**

CAN MEDICATION management truly make the difference for successful aging in place?

**Answer:**

There comes a time in everyone's life when the topic of remaining independent at home becomes the elephant in the room.[7] Whether it be for a partner, a parent, a sibling, or even for themselves, the baby elephant sits silently, growing daily until it can no longer be ignored. How did the sum of each minor accident or forgotten routine spiral so quickly into the proverbial dilemma sitting beside you? If it's happened to you then you're in good company. But what if there was a different way?

Of all the components it takes to age in place successfully, medication is amongst the most common concerns, yet one of the most complex to manage. It's also one of the most difficult conversations to have with someone else. Medication is personal, it's confidential, and it's self-monitored for most of our lives. Allowing someone else into that space takes trust that is built over the course of many conversations, not just a one-and-done. That truth applies whether it is between a provider

---

[7] https://www.merriam-webster.com/dictionary/elephant%20in%20the%20room

and their patient, a spouse caring for their significant other, or a nurse stepping in to assist with care.

As a nurse that has worked with older adults for over a decade in healthcare, teaching, training, and monitoring the fundamentals of wellness was the core of what I was trained to do. Did the treatment given, or the medication administered occur at the right time? Was it with the right person, in the right place, using the right dose, route, or method? Nursing is about balancing cause and effect, staying consistent, being aware of potential dangers, and both avoiding and planning for them. Detecting and effectively responding to changes in conditions at a rapid pace is the expectation of the nursing profession. So, what's the secret sauce to make all of that happen?

I can tell you that hands down, it comes down to excellent verbal and written communication, pre-planning, constant check-ins and follow-up, monitoring, adequate supply, ongoing safety evaluations, and especially ongoing education. Even with all those components running like a well-oiled machine, there are still no perfect outcomes in healthcare. Nor are there when it comes to growing older and making decisions surrounding the changes that go with it. Once I began working outside of acute care hospitals and sub-acute care nursing facilities, I moved into home and community-based programs. I began to hear different concerns that few on the care side were fully able to address. Time and time again, a caregiver or patient would report they were non-compliant with medications despite discharge orders being provided, instructions written on the medication from the pharmacy, or even after discussing medications with their prescriber. More times than not, it was due to insurance coverage, the inability to pay, physical or cognitive deficits, medication availability, and sometimes a simple lack of willingness to comply.

As I reflected on what happens daily in the hospital or a skilled nursing facility, I wondered how an individual could continue managing aging issues on their own at home. There is extensive documentation, monitoring, counting of medications, daily pharmacy orders, and full reports to the next shift of oncoming medical staff for continuity of care. A multi-disciplinary team led by a Medical Director, social workers, pharmacists, case managers, and around-the-clock nursing care. That led me to ask myself, how can we help people in their homes with limited to no support? Or even the typical person aging in place over the long term that had never been hospitalized? What happens as new health concerns arise or a current one advances?

I personally witnessed both my maternal and paternal grandparents face such contrasting circumstances as they were attempting to age in place. The ones that I thought were more affluent with greater resources both had the most difficulty with sad and compromising outcomes. However, my less financially fortunate ones were diligent planners, strategists, and realists. Those two grandparents lived their entire lives in their own homes, and both died peacefully there. How had they done it, I wondered. What did I not know about what went on behind the scenes? Why did their generation not allow "the children" to know what was going on, even when three of them were nurses?

During the COVID-19 pandemic, I was given the opportunity to train, study and sit for the licensed health insurance agent exam in my home state of Florida. I began contracting with many of the larger managed Medicare providers like Humana, United Healthcare, Aetna, and Anthem to name a few. I ultimately went on to work for Humana where I had the most wonderful mentors and teachers. I knew that understanding and working on the inside of both the healthcare (provider) and insurance (payor) worlds would help me learn how to be of service in ways that I could not before. And that I would have the opportunity to create a dialogue between the two that often saw each other as opposing sides.

When it comes to Medicare insurance, the complexity of the rules, special circumstances, election periods, appeals, what's covered, what's not, formulary exemptions, drug tiers, step therapy, penalties, copays, co-insurance, deductibles, and MOOPs… well, let's just say it was a mind-bender in the beginning. How could the typical older adult, much less a frail advanced-aged senior, manage this alone without extensive training? This is when I knew my call to do more, to integrate my experience between these two worlds, was going to be the most important work of my career up to this point.

Working as a clinical liaison in the community, I was often invited to functions at hospitals and healthcare facilities. There was one breakfast symposium that sticks out in my mind the most post-pandemic. The local case management department of a community hospital in my area called on all their vendor partners that assisted in discharging patients from the hospital back into the community. This was in later 2022 when the pandemic was being taken off the table as "the reason" for all failures, losses, outages, and omissions. This hospital was part of a large national chain spread across the United States, so when one loses, they all lose to some extent.

As the room filled and breakfast was served, the CEO of the hospital walked in. We all expected, as was the norm, for the head of case management to give updated protocol on what requirements you had to meet to work with and to be accepted as a preferred provider to their location. But instead, the CEO stood up and opened by thanking us all for our attendance and with an appeal for open dialogue from the gallery. What came next was a brave and innovative leadership move.

She turned on the overhead projector to display the fines, penalties, and losses for the last several quarters that had been imposed. The first words she spoke shattered the silence in the room with gasps of disbelief. Medicare had come after them, and it showed substantially in reimbursement payment reductions along with some hefty penalties. Hospitals face a myriad of challenges these days that almost seem insurmountable. But then again, you look at the amount of tax dollars moving through them, and you could easily lose sympathy. But when you personally know the good people working there, doing their best and it feels insurmountable from their duty stations, you rally around them.

The scathing topics of the morning surrounded two primary areas where they were penalized. First, the patient's length of stay in most of the departments exceeded the standard allowed by the patient's diagnosis. Second was hospital readmissions within 30 days of discharge and the fines that accompanied them. This has been a topic since 2012 when legislation was passed to tie payments for healthcare services to quality measures. The Hospital Readmissions Reduction Program (HRRP) is a Medicare value-based purchasing program that encourages hospitals to improve communication and care coordination to better engage patients and caregivers in discharge plans and, in turn, reduce avoidable readmissions. The program supports the national goal of improving health care for Americans by linking payment to the quality of hospital care.[8]

The bottom line is that if a patient is admitted for too long, the hospital would be fined. If the patient left too soon without a plan to keep them well and they get readmitted, they're fined. And would you believe one of the main reasons they found most of the senior population was being readmitted? You guessed it, medication!

Discharged patients often did not have an adequate supply to last until they could get the prescriptions filled at their pharmacy. Or they

---

8   https://www.cms.gov/Medicare/Medicare-Fee-for-Service-Payment/AcuteInpatientPPS/Readmissions-Reduction-Program; Paragraph 1:1-2.

discovered when they went to fill the new prescription or adjusted dose that their insurance plan doesn't cover it or that the copay is too high. Some had fallen into the dreaded "donut hole." Or more often than you think, they were confused about how to take the new prescriptions.

For many older adults, remaining independent in one's home depends on the ability to manage a complicated medication regimen.[9] I can't tell you how often I would talk to someone about the difference between what they were actually taking versus what was prescribed. I commend each of them for having the courage to share that they were non-compliant in the first place, but more so, for trusting me with the reasons why. These were not easy conversations for them even in the safe and trusted presence of a nurse.

I began to compile a list of the most common reasons I was given over the course of a few years. Do any of these sound familiar?

- I spilled my pill bottle when I tried to open it and lost a few. I'm out until the refill is due.
- I couldn't afford the copay for the new medicine the Doctor prescribed so I'm doubling up on my old prescription.
- I think I should take it twice a day, not three times as it says on the hospital papers.
- My doctor told me to take it every day, but I only take it when my legs get too swollen for my shoes. I know myself better than she does.
- I'm in the Medicare Part D donut hole coverage gap so I can't afford it.
- The plan I'm in this year doesn't cover this medicine and I'm not going to try a different brand that I know doesn't work for me.
- I can't get to the pharmacy as easily as I used to. I'll go when I'm feeling up to it.

---

9   Lewis A. Non-compliance: a $100 billion problem. The Remington Report. 1997;5(4):14–5.

- I either have to pay for food or my medicine in the last week of the month, I can't afford both.
- I think I took it, but I can't remember. Some of my pills look the same so I confuse them sometimes.
- I don't want my children to know what's going on, I don't want them to worry about me or to put me in a home.
- I'm running out much sooner than my prescription allows me to refill it.
- I have two full bottles that I haven't even used yet. Why is the pharmacy giving me so many?
- They make me feel bad, so I don't take them every day.

So, like I said in the beginning, what if there was a better way? Where would the path to better begin? I reached out to every provider and prescriber I know to ask what they hear, what they know, what they recommend, and what's missing to help lessen the burden of medication management at home.

I began to talk with neighbors, friends, and colleagues too. There seemed to be a common set of breakdowns no matter whom I spoke with. Prescribers felt in the dark because of a lack of meaningful data. Advocates and caregivers were most concerned with ease of communication, monitoring, supply issues, and ongoing education.

In preparation for this year's resources publication, I sat down with the current Executive Advisor to the Board of the Greater Tampa Bay Chapter of the NAIPC. Yvette joined our chapter for this very reason—to make sure all of those within her reach would have the information and resources from the provider perspective needed for improved outcomes.

Yvette Guzman, APRN is the CEO of Olive Health Florida. She is also the current Executive Advisor on the Board of the Greater Tampa Bay Chapter of NAIPC. Yvette's practice is a primary care mobile medical group that focuses on caring for people in their homes, whether that be a privately owned residence, an assisted living facility, or a group home. Her practice also works with skilled nursing centers to ease the transition from inpatient care back to home. I asked Yvette what she most wished, as a prescriber, that she could share with anyone reading this book or reaching out for resources to the NAIPC. Here's what she shared:

- Don't be afraid to ask questions about why you're starting a medication and how long you will need to be on it.
- Make sure you always have a current copy of your medication list. Make sure that list matches the bottles that you are using to take your daily medication.
- I see so many patients prescribed upwards of 10-20+ medications per day on an increasingly regular basis. Oftentimes, the patient or caregivers don't even know why it's been prescribed. It's possible that many of these could be reconciled and discontinued.
- Ask for a medication reconciliation and decrease review from your primary care provider. Let them work with specialists and external providers to complete the review on your behalf.
- Do not stop, add, or make changes to doses without a written plan from your medical provider.
- Being honest about what you're truly taking is very important. For example, if you were prescribed Metformin for blood sugar control to take daily, but rather than daily as prescribed, you only take it once or twice per week, when I see your lab work, I'll think you were taking the medicine as I wrote it for you. I'll then document in your medical record that you are taking the medicine as prescribed, and it created the lab results I'm seeing. I may make changes to your prescription based on this information.
- Another common medication that doesn't get taken as prescribed is Lasix also known as a water pill. It's typically prescribed to

control blood pressure or swelling in the legs. Often my senior patients will only take half, or sometimes none at all because it increases their need to urinate. Extra trips to the bathroom or using additional briefs may be the concern so they just cut it out. But they don't tell me, and we add additional medications to control blood pressure or believe that Lasix is not working.

And last, but not least, as a nurse working for years at in-patient facilities, assisted living, hospice, and home health as a clinical liaison, helping people to transition from one level of care to the next, here's what I recommend regarding medication management in the following situations.

## HOSPITALIZATION:

Remember that breakfast symposium I told you about? The outcome amongst all contributors to the solutions think tank agreed upon a few core actions.

- When you or a loved one is admitted to the hospital, you must start planning for the return home within the first 24 hours and so should the case manager. I know that sounds fast, but it's time to start a list on that very day.
- Will discharge be in a few days back home, or will more care be needed?
- Will the new medications be covered by your insurance plan?
- Will you be able to afford the copays?
- Is the hospitalist prescribing a brand-new medication that is difficult to get once outside of the hospital?
- Start the dialogue with your insurance company as soon as possible about new medications.
- Make sure that you have a list in your hand of the medications that you will be going home with.

- Get that list to your primary care provider as soon as possible. The hospital sends it out to whoever is supposed to be overseeing your care next, but I can't tell you how many times there are issues or delays with it getting there.
- Call your pharmacy or insurance company and get a cost estimate before you let them discharge you.
- Ask for Home Health if the plan is to return home and you feel teaching and training in the home environment is needed to be successful with new or changed medications.

## AT HOME:

When working with a client living at home, we build a full picture based on where the client and their support team are on the day they contact me. We get a baseline of what is working, what's not, and where they would like to see the situation at the end of our first meeting. We start to construct 30/60/90-day plans. We set goals for each timeline and begin by selecting individualized support methods to support them.

Realistic planning, knowing what resources you have available, and being honest about the ones you don't are the foundation for the most positive outcomes.

- Go to www.medicare.gov and start an account. Opt-in to receive updates and tips. Most of the information you can get from an insurance agent is listed there. But with a very strong word of caution, not understanding the complexity and how it works together can be catastrophic. You can also enter your medication lists into their planning tools if you feel confident doing it independently.

## Medication Matters

- If you opted to place your traditional Medicare benefit into a managed Medicare plan like an HMO, PPO, or PFFS plan, work directly with your insurance provider, especially when it comes to medications.
- If you have a Medicare Part D prescription drug plan, work directly with your provider and call as often as needed to discuss what's covered and how much it will cost.
- Find an **Unaffiliated Insurance Agent**[10] licensed for the state that you live in. They work for you, not for the insurance companies, for a preset agreed-upon flat fee.
- If you can't afford an unaffiliated agent, meet in person with a **local insurance agent** based on the recommendations of friends, family, and neighbors. Avoid working with insurance agents over the phone.
- Make sure the person you select to help you is available to you year-round and is an expert on getting your **needs analysis** completed including all your **medical providers**, their **locations, medical equipment, medical supplies, and all medications. Medicare Insurance Agents** are paid a commission by the insurance company they sign you up for. They are often incentivized to sell more of one carrier's plans than the other. Or they may not be appointed to offer you all of the different companies' plans out there.
- Make sure your insurance plan covers a **preferred in-network pharmacy** you have easy access to and that all your prescriptions are covered by that plan.
- Never trade your medical benefits in exchange for gimmicks to get free things from an insurance company. Nothing is ever free!

---

10 https://flsenate.gov/Laws/Statutes/2021/626.015 , 2021 Florida Statutes, 626.015, Line 20

It's always a trade-off. The more free or non-healthcare-related benefits you are promised, you often see a slimming or reduction in important benefits and freedom to choose providers when you need them, including pharmacies.

- Talk to your pharmacy about alternative packaging of your medications. Many offer pill packs broken down into daily doses. Most offer them by mail order delivery unless it is a controlled substance (like pain or anxiety pills). Just make sure wherever you choose to get medicine they are **in-network** or preferably a **preferred provider** in your insurance network.
- Hire a health coach or advocate that specializes in senior care if you can afford it. Make sure you understand their experience and background.
- Ask your primary care provider if they can refer you to a **home health** agency. If you have a new or changed medication due to a medical condition that was not being managed well, you may be eligible for additional medical oversight at home while you're adjusting.
- Use the technology and services available! Some devices may even be covered by your insurance provider. There are other types of machines that dispense pills, have motion sensors to detect trips to the bathroom, that give reminders to take medication, do vital signs checks and send a log to your doctor, prompt to bathe or perform routine hygiene, feed the cat, etc.
- For a list of resources and available services, please visit my webpage www.carecompassllc.com

# Gretchen "Gigi" Marquardt, PN, HMCT, LHIA

GRETCHEN "GIGI" MARQUARDT, PN has worked in the medical field for three decades as an EMT-I for the Fire Department, as a Nurse as a hospital-based clinical liaison, and in geriatric hospice and home healthcare. She is the founder and CEO of Care Compass LLC and LLC and Coherence University. Please visit **www.carecompassgroup.com** and **www.coherenceuniversity.org** to learn more.

Gigi is the founding member of the Greater Tampa Bay NAIPC, NAIPC©, and Chair of the Board. **The National Aging in Place Council®** is a senior support network that connects service providers with older adults, their families, and caretakers. The focus of the Greater Tampa Bay Chapter is to embody all Five Pillars of Healthy Aging, focusing on the dynamic landscape of healthcare in the bay area.

Gigi's desire for lifelong learning and service led her to attain her health insurance agent license focusing on Medicare and retirement plans. She elected to serve the community as an unaffiliated agent meaning that she works for the consumer, not the insurance companies. It has become her mission to educate consumers and to create a dialogue between health insurance plans and healthcare providers to work together for beneficiaries to age well.

Her heart for service, compassion, and a more loving way of living led her to pursue earning the prestigious **HeartMath Institute Coherence Advantage© Certified Trainer** credential. For more than 25 years, HeartMath Institute has been researching the heart-brain connection and learning how the heart influences our perceptions, emotions, intuition, and health using cutting-edge scientific research. HeartMath helps you tap into the power and intelligence of your heart – your heart's intuition – which awakens you to the best version of yourself. (www.heartmath.com)

Please visit https://carecompassgroup.com to learn more.

# "How Can I Get My Mom to Use Her Walker?"
## By Courtney Nalty

**Question:**

My mom needs a walker, but she doesn't want to use it. What can I say or do that will help her become more comfortable using it?

**Answer:**

This question comes up more than you would think!

Think about it. Since the time you started walking, you just get up and go. You have freedom and independence without a single thought. However, as you get older, now you must remember to grab an assistive device. Not just that, but that assistive device is not exactly the best-looking accessory.

Those thoughts and feelings that your mom is experiencing are what you need to have in mind from the beginning. It is important to have empathy for her situation. Put yourself in her shoes and realize what a disappointing change has come into her life. It is also a change that is unfairly ridiculed and mocked in society daily.

By having empathy, you can start the conversation with ease and thoughtfulness. This, in turn, will help with all the emotions.

Let me offer a script of a conversation for you:

"Mom, I notice you have not been using your walker lately. Why?"

Or

"Mom, I can understand that having a walker could make you feel sad or depressed. What can I do to make it feel better for you? I worry about you falling and injuring yourself."

From there you can suggest shopping online or going to a Durable Medical Equipment (DME) store. There are so many more options for walkers these days than there were just ten years ago.

If your mom is someone who has a unique fashion style, suggest finding a way to decorate the walker and add accoutrements to it, making it more personal.

For example, you could add items like these:
- a wicker basket
- a fanny pack
- a cup holder
- a phone holder
- a bicycle bell
- a bicycle light
- flowers and other flare

There are no rules to decorating a walker except for maintaining a safe, assistive device. Have fun with it. You might even suggest having her grandchildren help decorate it. Before you go shopping, or add personality to someone's walker, it is important to first consult with their Occupational Therapist (OT). An OT should be the person who suggested a walker in the first place because they assist with improving movement and gait.

When they work with a patient and evaluate them, they determine if someone can handle a walker with four rollers or two rollers. From there they can make recommendations and adjust the correct height of the walker. Sometimes just a height change or the number of wheels can make a world of difference.

If these ideas do not make a difference or help your mom, ask her who she currently misses the most. When she gives an answer, suggest she name the walker in honor of that person and take "them" for walks with her.

Still at a loss?

Ask if you, your mom, and their OT can have a conversation together about how to solve this problem. Being mindful and respectful of their say in the matter is so very important, even if they have mild cognitive impairment (MCI). Feelings are the one part of a person that are never lost or forgotten!

During this meeting you may even find that a walker is not the best assistive device. Maybe a scooter, a cane, or even walking poles are needed. In addition, it is possible that more PT (physical therapy) can improve their balance and gait.

If these solutions do not satisfy your mom's feelings, suggest meeting with her Primary Care Physician (PCP) to understand more regarding the needs of a walker. What are the physical reasons for an assistive device? Does she have a history of falls? Is she on a medication that affects her balance? Does she have an inner ear issue? Does she have Parkinson's Disease, ALS, or another chronic disease that will impact her ability to walk over time?

Sometimes understanding *why* the device is needed can make all the difference in the world!

So, let's recap:
1. Start the process with understanding your mom's feelings and come into the conversation with empathy.
2. Let your mom do all the talking first and validate what she is saying.
3. Meet with OT or PCP to understand the best type of walker or assistive device.

4. Write down all options and ideas, discuss together, and do what is best to make her happy.

Aging comes with many challenges, and adjusting to using a walker or assistive device is one of them. The more your mom understands why she needs it, and the more you can include her in the conversation, the better chance she has of adjusting to this change.

## Courtney Nalty

COURTNEY NALTY IS the founder of Generational Support, LLC, a caregiver consultancy, and resource guide founded in 2020.

In October of 2005, her journey began with taking a position in a CCRC. Over the 11 years of her service, she wore many hats. In 2017, she left the CCRC to work for a consulting firm that specializes in designing, developing, marketing, and concept ideation for the Active Adult real estate market.

A self-published author, she currently sells her two digital books (The Caregiver Toolbox and The Hospital Discharge Handbook) on her website, www.generationalsupport.com.

When not busy with work, she enjoys spending time with her husband, Will, and their three children, in and around her hometown of New Orleans, LA.

## Difficult Aging in Place Conversations

# Receiving and Accepting a Dementia Diagnosis

By Courtney Nalty

**Question:**

When your parent receives a dementia diagnosis, what are some of the things you can do to prepare for what's ahead and to support your parent in the meantime?

**Answer:**

You and your parent just left the doctor's office with a diagnosis of dementia. You have so many feelings right now, including a period of grief or ambiguous loss. The person, as you knew them, is no longer, but it is important to understand they really are still there. Memories and abilities will go, but feelings will remain. Acknowledge that grief is expected and healthy but be mindful not to do so in front of them.

From there you will recognize that action needs to be taken, but understanding what to do next can be overwhelming. To begin with, be sure to understand that type of dementia, a proper diagnosis can make a difference in the support the care team can provide and in turn, create a higher quality of life. You will also be able to understand and be prepared for the psychological, behavioral, and physical changes that you will observe over time.

Once you have answers and some direction, my first piece of advice is to do things in small bite sizes, and the best way is to create a check list.

**Build a Team of Support**

This team should include family, friends, neighbors, PCP, Attorney, Financial Advisor, Caregiver Consultant/Care Manager, and a Dementia Specialist (I'll explain this further down). Please note, this type of care cannot be done by just one person—you will burn out quickly.

**Secure a Power of Attorney (Medical and Financial)**

I suggest gathering the family, the Elder Law Attorney, and the Financial Advisor in one room when creating these documents, guaranteeing consistency, acceptance, and accountability.

Meet with the Financial Advisor to understand finances and insurance policies (especially Long-Term Care) to plan for future care and discuss what action needs to be taken to be financially comfortable.

**Educate Yourself**

Knowledge is power! A good place to start is by learning from the best, Teepa Snow (https://teepasnow.com/). She created the "Positive Approach to Care Program" and has been assisting families and communities for years. Teepa has also created a program that certifies professionals as a Dementia Specialist. These Dementia Specialists provide training, coaching, and support to care partners. By becoming educated early on with understanding dementia and caring for someone with dementia, you will gain valuable tools to endure this long journey—yes, this is a marathon.

# Receiving and Accepting a Dementia Diagnosis

Another resource is that of Lori La Bey, a former caregiver for her mom who created the Dementia Map (https://www.dementiamap.com/) and Alzheimer's Speaks Radio Podcast (https://alzheimersspeaks.com/). Both resources have won awards and praise from around the world.

## Hire a Caregiver Consultant/Care Manager

Hire a Caregiver Consultant/Care Manager to have on retainer to assist you when the unexpected happens. Whether it is a sudden ER visit or hospital stay, a need to downsize or move to a community, finding physicians or specialists (neurologist), or just a good shoulder to lean on, they do it all! They keep their finger on the pulse of all things in the aging industry and can step back and think outside of the box. By paying for their services up front you save time, energy, sanity, and money.

## Research and Visit Long Term Care Housing Options

Begin researching and visiting Long Term Care housing options now while your parent can have a say. Not to be Debbie Downer, but it is very likely that they will need 24-hour care at end-of-life, and with them having picked out a place when they were still capable will alleviate the stress and guilt you might experience during those days. I know from experience how difficult and stressful it becomes for family members when they are faced with an emergency and are overwhelmed with decisions. Be sure to visit Memory Care communities, Assisted Living, and Skilled Nursing—you will not know what will be needed until you are in the thick of it.

Are you starting to see a theme?! Preparation is important. It is something we humans do not excel at implementing, but aspiring to change that mindset and adapting will help you enjoy the benefits of having planned.

**Join a Care Partner Support Group**

Dementia does not just affect the person with the diagnosis, it affects the whole family. Care partners need support outside of each other. You can find support groups through the Alzheimer's Association, as well as religious organizations, some universities, and even virtual ones online. Some hospitals are now creating specialized Dementia Programs where the Social Workers provide support groups (ask your neurologist, or request to be seen by one if your parent is not yet.)

**Review and update documents**

Review and update documents regarding Living Will/ Advanced Directives, Medical Orders for Life-Sustaining Treatment (MOLST), POLST, and end-of-life wishes. Make sure the older adult has an updated photo ID and be sure to maintain a copy of it on hand.

**Inform your local police and fire departments.**

If they have begun to wander from home, inform your local Police and Fire department of the older adult with a copy of their picture ID, so that they are aware and knowledgeable when assisting during an emergency. In fact, the International Association of Chiefs of Police has a special initiative on this topic by providing education to police stations around the world on interacting with people with dementia and assisting their families.

## Look into engagement opportunities (day and respite programs)

Social interaction has been shown to slow down the disease. There are also dementia specialists who come into homes to provide therapeutic engagement that's tailored to their state of dementia. Also consider a 15-minute exercise per day consisting of reading aloud, doing simple math, and writing (visit www.strongermemory.com to learn more). There is so much living to be done after a diagnosis! Don't give up on them, in fact prolong their brain's abilities with mentally challenging activities, like crossword puzzles or a book group—not just reading a book but discussing it—staying physically active, socializing, and maintaining a proper diet are all things that can help.

## Don't be afraid to ask for help.

By all means don't be afraid to ask for help. We live in an era with so much research and knowledge, it would be fruitless to not tap into the many resources that are available in order to benefit from them. If you are interested in learning more, please check out my website listed in my bio on the next page.

Although a diagnosis of dementia creates a lot of uncertainty and mixed feelings, it is good to know that there are many resources and experts available to help. Follow the list above to make sure you've done everything you can to take care of your aging parent. During this time, they will need your help more than ever.

# Courtney Nalty

COURTNEY NALTY IS the founder of Generational Support, LLC, a caregiver consultancy, and resource guide founded in 2020.

In October of 2005, her journey began with taking a position in a CCRC. Over the 11 years of her service, she wore many hats. In 2017, she left the CCRC to work for a consulting firm that specializes in designing, developing, marketing, and concept ideation for the Active Adult real estate market.

A self-published author, she currently sells her two digital books (The Caregiver Toolbox and The Hospital Discharge Handbook) on her website, www.generationalsupport.com.

When not busy with work, she enjoys spending time with her husband, Will, and their three children, in and around her hometown of New Orleans, LA.

# "Am I Really Ready for Joint Replacement Surgery?"

By David T. Neuman, MD, FAAOS

**Question:**

As we age, our joints often deteriorate, and there comes a time when you might have to consider joint replacement surgery. What are the things you need to do to determine if it's time to have this kind of surgery? And how can you best prepare for it?

**Answer:**

As an orthopedic surgeon I treated and operated on people suffering with joint pain and loss of function. I remember patients expressing their frustration with their hip or knee. One person was playing his favorite sport, basketball, as a 24-year-old, and while coming down from a rebound landed awkwardly and tore his anterior cruciate ligament (ACL). He underwent a painful yet successful surgery and recovered enough to return to the basketball court, but with less confidence and skill. Recently, stair climbing and hiking was making his knee painful. He wanted to begin playing Pickleball but had increasing pain and stiffness in his knee. The lack of activity and altered lifestyle led to weight gain and less happiness in his life.

Another patient had jammed her right hip in a motor vehicle accident 20 years ago. She remembered a lot of pain and attending physical therapy after the injury. She recovered enough but had some lingering pain. The pain had recently become worse and was making it hard to stay active and enjoy golf and gardening. The loss of an active lifestyle made daily chores harder and increased her weight.

Both of these every day, regular people were suffering with chronic musculoskeletal (MSK) pain and loss of function. They were unable to perform their daily activities without pain and had lost their happiness when doing activities they loved. A recent survey conducted by the Centers for Disease Control and Prevention determined that people are developing new cases of chronic pain at higher rates than new diagnoses of diabetes, depression, or high blood pressure.[11] In 2019, the Rochester Epidemiology Project concluded that the most common reason for ambulatory visits to a medical provider was for MSK diseases.[12] If you have chronic MSK pain, you are certainly not alone!

The objectives of this chapter are to help aging people and their loved ones understand more about their bodies, specifically their musculoskeletal system (muscles, bones, and joints), and embrace successful aging. This may include undergoing joint replacement surgery (TJA), but the timing and expectations are important.

A joint is the coming together of two or more bones to create motion, and there are 360 joints in the human body The onset of chronic joint pain is due to an alteration of the normal architecture in the joint. A normal joint has smooth, cushioned surfaces and a lubricating fluid that minimizes friction to permit easy range of motion. When the smooth surfaces (articular cartilage/chondral surface) become rough, or when other soft tissues become damaged or degenerate, the joint begins to irritate the body causing inflammation.

---

[11] Rikard SM, Strahan AE, Schmit KM, Guy GP Jr. Chronic Pain Among Adults — United States, 2019–2021. MMWR Morb Mortal Wkly Rep 2023;72:379–385. DOI: http://dx.doi.org/10.15585/mmwr.mm7215a1.

[12] https://rochesterproject.org

# "Am I Really Ready for Joint Replacement Surgery?"

The four cardinal signs of inflammation: warmth (calor), redness (rubor), swelling (turgor) and stiffness (rigor). Quite commonly, the manifestation of some or all of these leads to loss of function (functio laesa).

I can remember the optimistic and relatively distraught patient asking me, "**How can I attempt to overcome chronic pain and continue to live an active life?**"

To successfully overcome challenges it takes understanding, empathetic guidance, and the right actions. Unfortunately, too many Americans (and people around the world) do not know what joints are made of, how they function, or how to care for them. It takes a desire to learn more about them so they can be cared for like teeth where we take preventive actions like flossing, brushing, getting check-ups, and using mouth wash. In addition, receiving treatment from an empathetic and compassionate doctor helps guide you to a better understanding. Finally, and perhaps most importantly, you must take matters into your own hands. Take small steps and use several different treatments to lower the feeling of pain and increase the function of an ailing joint. In one of my books, I describe the steps to help you overcome joint pain:

https://www.pop-doc.com/joint-preactive.html

Perhaps the most important step in this process is the last "E" in "PREACTIVE." "E" is for "Exercise!" Doing the right exercise at the right time will lessen the joint pain and allow you to function better and age with more happiness and grace.

Even after following these steps some people have joints that are simply too far gone. Despite efforts to overcome the chronic pain through perseverance and grit, they still struggle with the pain.

**Is it now time for joint replacement surgery?**

Joint replacement surgery is an open (as opposed to arthroscopic) surgery that involves cutting out the degenerated and diseased surfaces of the bones of a joint and replacing it with metal and/or plastic. Some constructs are ceramic, and others have no plastic in them. The plastic used is a high-density, cross-linked form of polyurethane. Some surgeons prefer and some patients benefit more with cemented (poly-methyl methacrylate) components. These variables and the "best" option for you depend on your health and are best discussed with your surgeon.

As per the American Academy of Orthopedic Surgery Total Joint Registry, in 2020 there were about 1.9 million hip and knee replacement surgeries done in America, by about 1.9 thousand different surgeons. These procedures are quite common and are great treatment options when they are timed right and performed by an appropriate surgeon. If you tried to overcome joint pain by being PREACTIVE and underwent less invasive treatments from your doctor (injection therapy, nerve ablation, and arthroscopic surgery), then it may be time for the next step: total joint replacement surgery. A surgery such as this, done well, can last anywhere from 10-30 years. Therefore, before you become less healthy, and chronologically "older" and less able to heal, perhaps now is the time. On average, people are living until they are in their late seventies (slightly falling over the last few years), and you may strive to live longer and be present to see your grandchildren get married. Therefore, if the pain is too much, and you still have the strength and desire to live, by 65 years old you should take the next step in overcoming your chronic joint pain.

# "Am I Really Ready for Joint Replacement Surgery?"

If the thoughts are there and you struggle daily due to chronic MSK pain, you have internal strength (mental and biological), and the social support, it is time to go for it.

**But who is the right surgeon for you?**

I practiced Sports Medicine and surgical arthroscopy after spending a year of fellowship training. Arthroscopy is a specialty within orthopedic surgery that addresses joint pathology using small incisions instead of large cuts to the skin. Through these incisions a camera (scope) is put into the joint (arthro) and then work is done using small instruments as the inside of the joint is viewed on a monitor. I am Board Certified in my profession, and that means that I have been assessed with a test, evaluated by my peers, and credentialed by a governing body (The American Board of Orthopedic Surgeons).

Total joint replacement surgery (joint arthroplasty) is a complex surgery that takes a team to successfully complete. In addition, it takes a facility that can handle this type of surgery and the right one is one that performs many TJAs per year. The lead surgeon is the head of the surgery and is responsible for assuring your safety and completing the technical aspects of the surgery. I recommend finding a total joint surgeon who is fellowship trained in joint arthroplasty. They should perform the specific surgery you need (hip, knee, ankle, shoulder, elbow, wrist) many times a month. They should have at least five years of experience (repetitions) doing the surgery you need. Studies reveal that having total joint surgery at facilities that do more of them, with a surgeon who performs more of them, leads to a higher likelihood of success.

When patients and people ask me about this type of surgery (I have a thorough understanding of the inflammatory response that ensues after the controlled trauma a person endures as a result of surgery), they are often curious about what to expect during the post-operative course. I advise them that what they do before the surgery can help set them up for success after the surgery.

Recently, there is a trend encouraging TJA doctors (and other doctors who care for patients with chronic joint pain) to have their patients undergo physical therapy before the surgery. This is called "prehab" or pre-habilitation. I am a strong advocate of this option. After TJA, a person basically has to learn how to walk again. The stronger the person's muscles are around the operated joint, the more quickly they will regain control of their new joint and be able to transition back to a life they deserve and desire.

**However, what tips, thoughts, and suggestions can I offer that help a person (or their family) understand what to expect after a hip or knee (or ankle) replacement surgery?**

Surgical skills have improved over the last decade thanks in part to new technology, better teaching methods, and more surgeries being done (increased repetitions). More so, some of these TJA surgeries are now being done in an outpatient (no overnight beds) setting and some select patients can even return home the night of surgery. It is an amazing thought and concept that was hardly possible 15 years ago!

No matter where the surgery takes place, before the surgery it is important to prepare a plan for the first few weeks after surgery. After the patient is stable and awake after surgery there are options as to where they go: remain in the hospital for a few days, rehabilitation facility, short-term nursing facility, their home, or family member's home. Wherever it is, being prepared with food, accessories, adapted bathroom/bedroom items, is quite important.

Surgery is an act of controlled trauma. Cutting into the body, sawing bones, hammering implants, stopping bleeding, and closing the incision are all done in control. However, this still leads to an inflammatory

## "Am I Really Ready for Joint Replacement Surgery?"

response. Surgeons and anesthesia doctors (the medical specialists involved with controlling pain during and immediately after a TJA surgery) should discuss the "best" option for you.

Some surgeons believe in utilizing durable medical equipment after TJA surgery. These can be devices like braces, cold therapy apparatus or continuous passive motion machines. All serve different purposes and are surgeon dependent. Sometimes your insurance dictates what devices are permitted after the surgery.

For lower extremity joint replacement surgery (hip, knee, ankle) a person has to learn how to essentially walk again. In our joints the soft tissues have nerves that communicate with the brain and with each other. Nerves (I like to think of them as tiny electrical wires that send and receive impulses from the brain) allow us to feel, physically move, and maintain our balance and coordination. When the bones are cut and some soft tissues in the joint removed during TJA, some of the nerves are also cut, compressed, stretched, or damaged. Therefore, putting pressure on a replaced joint will not feel like it did before it was replaced. For many who suffered with longstanding chronic joint pain the new joint will feel simply amazing. However, assistive devices such as wheelchairs, crutches, braces, or canes are often used for a period of time until your balance is restored, the surgical pain subsides, and your muscles wake up and support you again.

Do you ever have an odd feeling in your ankle after you sit on it for a period of time (and it begins to ache, cramp, or fall asleep)? Those are the nerves around the ankle responding to the stimulus of bearing your weight. If the nerves had been put to sleep before you sat on your ankle, they would not feel the weight and would not give you the perception of pain. I thought about this when I operated and would therefore knock out the function of nerves by injecting an anesthetic around the skin I was about to cut (and inject the joint before I entered it with a camera and instruments). In addition, I would inject the skin (and joint) after the surgery was over in order to prolong the nerves' dysfunction. I advise that you ask your surgeon about this technique and whether or not this is part of their protocol. After surgery, this technique may help the pain return at a slower pace and to a less-severe level.

During the first few days after surgery, calming the pain, controlling the swelling, and becoming more mobile is definitely advocated. Your surgeon may have handouts or give verbal instructions about how to achieve this. Opioids are powerful and addictive medications and can become deadly. If you feel you "must have" them, I strongly think you should stop them by day three. I find that (depending on your stomach and liver function) Extra-strength Tylenol with or without an anti-inflammatory medication (with food) controls pain well.

In order to control swelling I prefer cryotherapy (ice with compression) intermittently since it diminishes the feeling of pain, lessens swelling, and lowers the quantity of substances in the joint that bring on the feeling of pain. Elevating the joint (raising the knee or ankle over the heart, but it is harder to raise the hip over the heart unless the bed or couch can tilt) helps coax the fluid back to your body as opposed to down to your toes.

Remaining in bed is a set up for stagnation and weakness. Stagnation of blood flow can lead to a blood clot and is quite painful and dangerous. Getting out of bed within the first 6-12 hours after TJA is very important. Standing up, with help, is also strongly advocated in the first 6-12 hours after TJA surgery.

Ambulation assistance with the help of a professional (physical therapist, nurse, aide) is advocated until your muscles wake up and your leg has the control it needs to prevent a fall. Digital therapy is a great way to supplement formal physical therapy. Physical therapy takes place as an in-patient, out-patient, or within your home. However, nothing beats you having the drive, knowledge, and desire to "get better." Doing the right exercises on a daily basis, and building a routine of gaining strength, balance, and coordination will optimize your outcomes from surgery.

I hope reading this chapter has increased your understanding of what to expect when you want to choose surgery (TJA) as a treatment to overcome chronic joint pain. I believe you have the desire and power to smile more, feel less pain, and have the ability to spend more time with friends, family, and loved ones. Staying active with less pain definitely helps a person age gracefully and increase their Health Span (the ability to live independently and without being reliant on devices, pills, or others to successfully complete activities of daily living). Remember, you are not simply a painful joint but rather a whole person. Assessing your current lifestyle and making small changes can lead to personal success and more fun times with your friends, family, and loved ones. Being mindful, getting enough rest, staying hydrated, and eating right are all important aspects of aging gracefully. Embrace this: "Knowledge + Action = Power!" and "Healthier Joints Make Happier People!"

## David T. Neuman, MD

DAVID NEUMAN IS Board Certified Orthopedic Surgeon, clinical director of NY Sportscare, TEDx speaker, Executive Director of a non-profit, internationally published author, and international speaker. David founded and created a digital therapeutic company, Pop-Doc. Pop-Doc creates and designs Corrective Exercise Therapy programs for populations wanting to 'Exercise Again' and age gracefully.

www.pop-doc.com

# FINANCE & FAMILY

# When Is the Right Time to Claim Social Security

By Tara Ballman

**Question:**

My neighbor said I should take Social Security right when I turn 66, but I heard I can get more if I wait and file a claim using my ex-husband's income info later. Is there a magic age at which I should aim to get the maximum benefits? I'm about to retire and I want to get back all the money I put into Social Security.

**Answer:**

This is not a simple question to answer because there is no perfect claiming strategy. Each individual and situation are different. The perfect claiming strategy for your neighbor could be the worst option for you.

Although there is one consistent in every scenario – proper planning.

Generally speaking, the longer you wait to claim, the larger your benefit will be. If you retire at age 62, the earliest possible Social Security retirement age, your benefit will be lower than if you wait.

Higher lifetime earnings result in higher benefits. If there were some years you didn't work or had low earnings, your benefit amount may be lower than if you had worked steadily.

As you think about your Social Security claim, I challenge you to be realistic about your current and future situation. Consider your health and longevity expectations as well as your financial means. Think about the funds you need versus when – and why – you will need additional income. And it also depends on your marital status and your concern for survivor benefits.

Before we dive into the "magic age" part of your question, let's review the Social Security program and how it works.

**Who is Eligible to Collect Social Security?**

Individuals who have earned 40 credits in the program, which equates to roughly 10 years of contributing to Social Security through employment, can receive Social Security retirement benefits as early as age 62.

Spouses of those who have earned Social Security entitlement are also eligible to receive benefits, as well as former spouses married at least 10 years. Survivors of deceased retirees must be at least 60 – or 50 if disabled – which includes both current and former spouses, as well as dependent children.

Here's something most people don't know: If you are caring for a dependent parent with a lower Social Security benefit than yours, it is possible for your parent to get your higher amount.

**How is the Benefit Calculated?**

Knowing what Social Security considers your full retirement age is critical in your decision on when to file your claim. Full retirement age is the point at which you receive 100% of the benefits available to you. In some scenarios, waiting just one additional month to submit your claim will result in an increase in payments.

## AGE TO RECEIVE FULL SOCIAL SECURITY BENEFITS

| Year of Birth | Full Retirement Age |
|---|---|
| 1943-1954 | 66 |
| 1955 | 66 and 2 months |
| 1956 | 66 and 4 months |
| 1957 | 66 and 6 months |
| 1958 | 66 and 8 months |
| 1959 | 66 and 10 months |
| 1960 and later | 67 |

NOTE: People born on January 1 of any year, refer to the previous year.

Source: Social Security - https://www.ssa.gov/

Full retirement age varies depending on the year you were born. If you were born before 1960, your full retirement age is 66 and some number of months depending on the exact year. If your birth year was 1960 or later, your full retirement age is 67. (ssa.gov)

Collecting Social Security before your full retirement age will result in your benefits being cut. For example, if you turn age 62 in 2023, your monthly benefit amount would be about 30% lower than it would be at your full retirement age of 67.

Another area to consider is your retirement date. Some people stop working before age 62. But if they do, the years with no earnings probably mean a lower Social Security payment.

Conversely, if you could wait and collect Social Security after your full retirement age, you're going to get more – up to 132% of your average index monthly earnings.

The Social Security program has your lifetime earnings record which it receives annually from the IRS. The IRS tells Social Security how much you earn, but only up to the maximum payroll tax each year, also known as the contribution and benefit base. At the time of publication in 2023, the payroll tax cap was $160,200.

Social Security takes your annual earnings from over your lifetime, adjusts each year for inflation (which also varies per year), and calculates your earnings based upon today's dollars, not on the actual dollar amount you earned in those years.

This calculation is based on the 35 years in which you earned the most income and divides that number by 420 – the number of months in 35 years – which gives you your average index monthly earnings.

The calculation process can get a bit complicated to explain after that point. But if you were doing a "back of the napkin" calculation, the monthly benefit comes out at roughly 40% of your average index monthly earnings.

**Will I Get Back What I Paid Into Social Security?**

A Social Security Advisor for a nonprofit focused on financial education is repeatedly asked, "When will I break even when it comes to paying into Social Security versus receiving payments?"

"I've looked at this," he said. "If you wait until your full retirement age to claim, by 78 you will have collected the same amount of money as if you had collected or started benefits at age 62. Similarly, if you wait until 70 to claim, you're going to break even at about 81. If you wait until 70 versus claiming at 62, you're breaking even at 81, and if you wait until 70, instead of claiming at your full retirement age, you're going to break even about 83."

**Working and Collecting Social Security – Before Full Retirement Age**

Many are not aware that if you take Social Security benefits at age 62, you are limited to the amount of income you can earn. Social Security has an earnings limit for those who collect Social Security before reaching full retirement age. In 2023, the earnings limit is $21,240. Once you reach your full retirement age, the earnings limit no longer applies.

If you exceed the earnings limit, Social Security will withhold $1 in benefits for every $2 you are over the limit. And you'll receive an overpayment notice which could results in repaying thousands of dollars.

## Spousal Benefits

Spouses who never worked or have low earnings can get up to half of a retired worker's full benefits. If your benefits as a spouse – or a former spouse if you were married at least 10 years and divorced at least 2 years – are higher than your own retirement benefit, you'll receive an amount equal to the spouse's higher benefit.

For example, a person qualifies for a retirement benefit of $1,250 and a spouse's benefit of $1,400. At full retirement age, they will get their $1,250 retirement benefit, plus Social Security will add $150 from their spouse's benefit, for a total of $1,400. If the person takes the retirement benefit before full retirement age, both amounts will be reduced.

## Taxes on Social Security Payments

If your combined income (50% of your benefit amount plus any other earned income) exceeds $25,000/year filing individually or $32,000/year filing jointly, you will pay federal income taxes on your benefits. It is possible for Social Security to withhold money for taxes if you ask.

## Planning for *YOUR* Social Security

It is possible to preview an estimate of your personal retirement benefits and see the effects of claiming your benefits at different ages. If you don't have a personal Social Security account, it is easy to create one at www.

ssa.gov/myaccount with your Social Security number (SSN), a valid US mailing address, and an email address.

**SSA My Account Link**

It is recommended that you apply for Social Security about four months before you want your benefits to start. For example, if you want your first check in April, you should:
- Apply in November, December, January, February, or March.
- Indicate March in the application.
- First check arrives in April.

You'll need some basic documents to complete the application:
- Proof of your Social Security number (SSN).
- Birth certificate.
- W-2 forms or self-employment tax return for the previous last year.
- Your military discharge papers, if applicable.
- Your spouse's birth certificate and SSN.
- Proof of US citizenship or lawful alien status if you (or a spouse applying for benefits) were not born in the United States.

If you have any questions about the process, Social Security offers assistance in multiple ways. With an online account, you can apply for retirement, disability, and Medicare benefits. You can also check the status of an application (or appeal) and print a benefit verification letter. If you are unable to access their online system, call the national hotline at 1-800-772-1213 for help. They can schedule you for a phone appointment or in-person appointment at your local Social Security office.

There are also many nonprofits that provide education related to Social Security. I always recommend the AMAC Foundation (www.amacfoundation.org), which provides free counseling for retirees and pre-retirees on all issues related to Social Security (and Medicare). Several of their advisors have earned accreditation as National Social Security Advisors (www.nationalsocialsecurityassociation.com), which has an online searchable directory if you'd like to find someone in your area.

**AMAC Foundation**

**NSSA**

## Questions to Consider

**Are you still working?**

If you plan to continue working while receiving Social Security benefits, there are limits on how much you can earn each year between age 62 and full retirement age and still get all of your benefits.

Social Security will recalculate your benefit amount to give credit for months you did not receive a benefit because you continued working. Once you reach full retirement age, your earnings do not affect your benefits.

**What is your life expectancy?**

When Social Security first began paying monthly Social Security benefits in 1940, life expectancies were much different!

You must consider your family history and lifestyle when thinking about your life expectancy. If you come from a family with long-life expectancies, you may need extra money in later years.

Your life expectancy affects your retirement planning decisions. Knowing this, helps you determine whether you should start receiving your benefits at age 62, or wait until age 70 to receive a higher payment.

You can view the average life expectancy rate based on your birthdate on the Social Security website at www.ssa.gov/OACT/population/longevity.html

## Do you still have health insurance?

Although there are exceptions, most people will not be covered by Medicare until they reach age 65. Are you still covered under an employer-provided plan?

| Year of Birth | Full (normal) Retirement Age 1. | Months between age 62 and Full Retirement Age 2. | AT AGE 62 | | | |
|---|---|---|---|---|---|---|
| | | | A $1000 retirement benefit would be reduced to | The retirement benefit is reduced by 4. | A $500 spouse's benefit would be reduced to | The spouse's benefit is reduced by 5. |
| 1943-1954 | 66 | 48 | $750 | 25.00% | $350 | 30.00% |
| 1955 | 66 and 2 months | 50 | $741 | 25.83% | $345 | 30.83% |
| 1956 | 66 and 4 months | 52 | $733 | 26.67% | $341 | 31.67% |
| 1957 | 66 and 6 months | 54 | $725 | 27.50% | $337 | 32.50% |
| 1958 | 66 and 8 months | 56 | $716 | 28.33% | $333 | 33.33% |
| 1959 | 66 and 10 months | 58 | $708 | 29.17% | $329 | 34.17% |
| 1960 and later | 67 | 60 | $700 | 30.00% | $325 | 35.00% |

1. If you were born on January 1st, you should refer to the previous year.
2. If you were born on the 1st of the month, we figure your benefit (and your full retirement age) as if your birthday was in the previous month. If you were born on January 1st, we figure your benefit (and your full retirement age) as if your birthday was in December of the previous year.
3. You must be at least 62 for the entire month to receive benefits.
4. Percentages are approximate due to rounding.
5. The maximum benefit for the spouse is 50 percent of the benefit the worker would receive at full retirement age. The percent reduction for the spouse should be applied after the automatic 50 percent reduction. Percentages are approximate due to rounding.

# Tara Ballman

TARA BALLMAN IS a nationally recognized aging in place expert who is passionate about connecting and supporting professionals serving older adults. She is an internationally known author of three books on financial retirement issues and authored the transportation section of NAIPC's first publication, *Aging in Place Conversations: What Industry Experts Have To Say*.

For years, Tara and her family struggled through the evolving stages of her father's declining health. Unexpected illnesses, unforeseen situations, and a fear of the future was their reality, with so many questions and nowhere to turn. After her father passed, she had a desire to help other families navigate through the stages of aging and proactively plan for future needs, regardless of what life throws at them.

Tara currently serves as Executive Director for the National Aging in Place Council, where she brings professionals and communities together to champion aging in place through collaboration, education, and advocacy.

www.linkedin.com/in/taraballman

www.taraballman.com

www.ageinplace.org

# The Probate Process as it Relates to Real Estate "And This, Too, Shall Pass"

By Peter Demidovich

**Question:**

When a family member passes away, besides dealing with the loss and grief of a loved one, there are responsibilities that come with settling the affairs of an estate. Especially if there is Real Estate to manage maintain and liquidate. How do I navigate the Probate process in the surrogates' court system while handling other heirs and family as the appointed Executor?

**Answer:**

Probate is an administrative process that most people are unfamiliar with until they are forced to learn about it in a crash course and all at once. It usually comes at a very stressful time when a family member passes away. This is why most people seek guidance and help navigating the process. In full disclosure, I am not an attorney, and I am not giving legal advice. Every family's situation is different. I am going to give a wide overview to encourage thought and conversation as to what to avoid and to understand the process a little better. The laws are different from state to state and even counties within the same state vary in nature. I am in New York and will be covering specifically how to transfer Real Property and to explain how the Probate process works. I will provide tips and suggestions that I have learned through my almost 30 years as a real estate sales agent and office manager that will give you guidance to make your personal situation easier. Filing for probate is obviously an action that takes place after a loved one has passed away. Ideally, discussing your wishes with family and sound legal and financial planning, everyone involved should know what to expect when the inevitable moment arrives.

**Probate as defined by the American Bar Association:**

"Probate is the formal legal process that gives recognition to a will and appoints the executor or personal representative who will administer the estate and distribute assets to the intended beneficiaries."[13]

## Trusted Advisors, Legal Council

Whether you are the appointed trustee, executor, or discussing family planning and setting up final wishes and a will, it is imperative to work with a trusted financial planner and an attorney that is versed in the probate process. Although you do not NEED an attorney to file for probate, it would be my suggestion to seek sound legal advice before you start. It would also be my suggestion to speak with a tax professional and a licensed Realtor® if there is real estate involved in the estate. By planning ahead, you can have a clear plan on transferring ownership of real property and tax strategies that will save the estate thousands of dollars if put into place early. It is never too early or too late to be prepared and start planning.

---

[13] https://www.americanbar.org/groups/real_property_trust_estate/resources/estate_planning/the_probate_process/#:~:text=Probate%20is%20the%20formal%20legal,assets%20to%20the%20intended%20beneficiaries.

# The Probate Process as it Relates to Real Estate

## Who Needs to File Probate?

First, if the decedent was legally married, in most cases the surviving spouse will have the right of survivorship. Do not assume, however, that this is the case. The laws are different in each state regarding tenancy by the entirety, joint tenancy, and tenants in common. Also, when it comes to real estate, are both spouses' names on the deed? I see this happen often. Years ago, it was common to have the deed to a house only in the husband's name. Also, was the deed recorded correctly if the owners refinanced a loan or was there a second marriage that names were changed years ago? Whether there was a valid will in place (called Testate) or no will at all (Intestate), the family still might have to file for probate. There were some very famous and wealthy individuals that you would think would have planned their estate in advance to keep them out of probate court. Aretha Franklin, The artist known as Prince, and Steve Job's estate (Apple Computers) all had to be Probated for one reason or another. It really depends on several things:

1. Was the estate placed in a trust?
2. What was addressed and covered in the will? All assets including investments, real estate, and any belongings in the county that the decedent lived in or anywhere else in the United States?
3. The value of the assets. There is a minimum threshold. If the total value of the estate is under the threshold, you might not have to file or be able to file a small estate expedited version of probate. This amount is different from county to county. A total amount could range from $25,000 to $50,000 but check with your county's surrogate court office.

## Role of an Executor/Personal Representative

As the executor or Personal representative of an estate, you are agreeing to be responsible for not only the liquidation and disbursement of assets of the decedent, but also to make sure all the debts are paid as well. Once authorized, you can open a bank account in the name of the estate and will be able to act as the representative of the estate. You will be accountable for all of the accounting and all of the estate's paperwork.

## Filing probate/opening probate/getting authority

The actual filling process is administrated by the county in which the deceased person last resided. Typically, court proceedings are initiated by the executor of an estate or someone that has been named in the deceased person's will, or by a relative of someone who has passed away without a will. It is a function of the county surrogates court and not unlike filing for divorce or filling out paperwork to register a car, but a bit more time consuming and complex. You will need the name and address of the person who died (called the decedent), a certified copy of the death certificate, the name and address of the decedent's husband or wife, children, grandchildren, and parents. If their parents are deceased, then you will need the name and address of the decedent's siblings. If the siblings are deceased, then you need the name and address of the sibling's children. You also need the original will if the decedent had a will, the names and addresses of people mentioned in the will, a list of all assets (I discuss real property below) including bank accounts, investment accounts, insurance policies, cars, boats, and any other vehicles. You will need account numbers and vehicle identification numbers for all of these. Document a list of all the decedent's assets at the time of death.

Once probate has been filed correctly, it will take several weeks to several months to receive the executor/administrators' letters of authorization. The court will schedule a hearing to preside over the process of probating the will or administering the estate and will authenticate the last will and testament. Once received, this grants the executor the authority to act for the estate.

## Property Valuation

The county will want a complete valuation of the decedent's assets AT THE TIME OF DEATH. This is important to take note of because quite often I will get asked to do a "current" market evaluation for a property that has been left vacant by the deceased for many years. It is certainly possible to do, but it takes a little bit more work on the multiple listing service to find sold comparable properties from years gone by. This is what I do as a Realtor®. I provide free market information, supported by comparable sales in the local area to come up with a current value or "marketing" price for a house or property. I provide a full report and will make that comparative market analysis (CMA) available to whomever the Executor and attorney direct me to. I offer this service at no cost, in the hopes that when the property is ready to be listed for sale, that the estate will utilize my services. There are circumstances however, that an estate may require a written appraisal.

## How Long Does It Take?

The next step is when will you receive your "Letters of Administration?" This is such a difficult question to answer. Was there a valid will? Is the will being contested by anyone? How many heirs are addressed in the will? Have they all been contacted? Are there business assets owned with business partners? But mostly it is dependent on the county court system. Once all the probate paperwork is filed, correctly, it is really all in the hands of whatever county you filed it in. It should take anywhere from a few weeks to several months depending on the caseload of the court system. There are plenty of things, however, that you can do and prepare for while you are waiting for authority. This is a big mistake that I see quite often that the family does nothing with a decedent's house and belongings for months and sometimes years. If there is a house to sell, this is the time to engage with an experienced Realtor® to guide you how to properly "stage" the house. They will be a resource as to what repairs should be made, if any, what to leave and what items should be removed and what can be donated. While you do need a full accounting of all valuable belongings, you can prepare by doing a decluttering of the house, which can be very time-consuming. Take advantage of the lag time while waiting for letters of administration.

## Paying Bills and Taxes

All the outstanding bills for the estate will have to be paid, eventually. There are however ways to negotiate lowering outstanding credit card and medical bills on a case-to-case basis. If there is liquid capital (money in unrestricted bank accounts) and you have the authority to access it, these funds can be used to pay bills. A full written accounting should be kept for any transactions on behalf of the estate. The real estate taxes will have to be paid on time to avoid penalties. Unfortunately, the county doesn't care that someone died, they just want their money. Thousands of houses a year are foreclosed on in this country for not paying real estate taxes! If there is no money available from the estate or all of the assets are tied up in investments or the real estate, to make regular payments, then the real estate taxes will be paid out of the proceeds of the sale of the house. Please keep in mind that if the decedent had any tax exemptions (senior exemption, veterans' exemption, etc.) those will be removed from the tax roles as of the date of death and will be due retroactively. Estate taxes and capital gains taxes might be/will be due but there is no way to answer this question generally and is dependent on your state, what was held in the estate, and your financial situation. Please discuss this with your accountant.

## Distributing Assets and Closing the Estate

Once all the bills have been paid and the assets distributed or liquidated, the estate can be closed. This is the final accounting for all the assets and debts that were owned and were owed by the decedent. The Surrogate's court will make a final determination on who the rightful heir or heirs are, the validity of the will, and should anyone have rights to contest the will. Once again, I suggest that you should consult a tax professional to guide you through how to handle the IRS regarding payments from an inheritance.

## Tips and Suggestions

Utilize professionals! I can't stress enough that hiring the right professionals for the right job will save you time and money in the long run! I have helped dozens of executors and families who are local, as well as those who live out of state or hours away from where the property is here in New York. Once they realize that I provide a service that will take care of whatever needs to be done. While I always suggest having legal counsel, the attorney you hire will most likely never see or go inside the house that needs to be sold. I work alongside your attorney and act as a bridge between our client and a list of suggested vendors and contractors to make sure the house is seen in the best light possible and maximize the value of the estate. Whether providing local licensed and insured plumbers, electricians, roofers, and landscapers, or helping to coordinate tag sales, donations, shipping personal belongings elsewhere, and cleaning a vacant house in preparation for sale, they all say: "I should have called you sooner." I will get done in a short period of time what will take most executors a month of Sundays to accomplish so they can get on with their lives and the things that are most important to them.

Act quickly and put a plan in motion. Especially if there is real estate in the estate, and if is left vacant. Besides for the obvious paying taxes, maintenance, and upkeep for an empty house, there is always the possibility of damage and intruders. Through the years I have encountered intruders of the furry kind (raccoons, squirrels, mice, and rats) who just seem to know when a house is vacant, and human intruders, which are much more difficult to get rid of! Burglars can break into any house, but a house left vacant for a long period of time can also invite squatters. House squatting seems to be on the rise in the last few years, and professional criminals know how to "work the system." I have seen cases where squatters have moved into a house, changed the names on the cable service and sometimes utilities into their names (now you can't shut it off) and created a fake lease to prove they have the right to live there! Post no trespassing signs, then the police can arrest them right away. Once they "settle in" it becomes a civil matter, and the police will tell you to evict them. That will take months, cost thousands of dollars and potentially leave you with a destroyed house.

Make your intentions known. Having a will should take care of the large items that are part of an estate, but far too often smaller items are overlooked and or not addressed in a will. Things like jewelry and furniture and other family heirlooms can be a point of contention for surviving family members left to argue about. Have it spelled out in writing!

Bank accounts should have cosigners or executors listed on the accounts. Access to accounts could be frozen after the date of death leaving that estate with no funds to maintain a house for months. This will force the heirs to spend their own money to pay bills and for repairs that need to be done. If funds are needed and there are no other options, there are companies that will write a short-term loan to the executor, based on the expected proceeds from the estate.

## The Probate Process as it Relates to Real Estate

Safety deposit boxes with only one name on the account and no beneficiary will keep belongings safe. So safe that NO ONE ELSE will be able to get into them! This situation happened to me and my family personally when my father passed away. He had a safety deposit box with his will, the family home mortgage satisfaction, and some gold coins in it. We had the key but were not able to access it because it was only in his name. Sometime later we were able to inventory the box, by providing a death certificate (and with bank staff present) and couldn't empty it until authority was granted to my mother. It was unnecessary added stress that could have been avoided.

Plan and update your will. Choose your executor. Please keep in mind that a will you create today might not be looked at for years to come. Sometimes people who were named as executor to a will pass away before being granted that authority. You might consider choosing a successor or co-executors.

Homeowners insurance is written in the name of the homeowner. When the person dies, that policy might not still be in effect. Check with your insurance company. You might have to get a new policy or get a vacant home insurance policy if there is no one living there.

Get extra copies of the death certificate. Every bank account, credit card, utilities, and transaction that you make as executor will request one. They will want an original, not a copy. Most funeral homes will provide them at your request.

For additional information, go to this link: https://longislandprobateresource.com/probate-faq-glossary/

# Peter Demidovich,
## Seniors Real Estate Specialist (SRES)

PETER HAS BEEN A Licensed Associate Real Estate Broker in New York since 1996. First as a successful Sales Agent, then as an office manager for several of the largest real estate companies on Long Island, helping hundreds of customers and clients buy and sell real estate in New York as well as a national reach through his connections with many associations. Having served for 20 years as a Director for the Long Island Board of Realtors and chairing many of its committees including Bylaws, Legislative, Professional Standards, and Vice President of Executive. Having also been awarded "The Realtor of the Year Award" in 2008 from a membership of almost 30,000. Concurrently having served on the Board of Directors for the New York State Association of Realtors (NYSAR) and the National Association of Realtors (NAR), as well as many committees through the years. Peter has the Certified Residential Broker Manager (CRB) designation, as well as the Short Sale & Foreclosure

# The Probate Process as it Relates to Real Estate

Resource Certification (SFR) and Senior Real Estate Specialist (SRES). Peter earned the Eagle Scout Rank in 1983 and has remained active with his local Boy Scout Troop 106 and committee as well as receiving "The Good Deed Award" from Suffolk County Council of Boy Scouts in 2008. Other associations include Past President of the Huntington Historical Society, Huntington Chamber of Commerce and Past Exalted Ruler of The Benevolent Protective Order of Elks Lodge #1565.

Currently Peter works for Realty Connect USA since the company's inception in 2009 and focuses his time on working with Attorneys and helping families and surviving spouses navigate the complexities of their loved one's estate and probated properties as a Certified Probate Expert (CPE). Utilizing his experience and skills as an SRES, Peter enjoys helping seniors "Rightsizing" their home whether it be with family or one of the many aging in place options locally or across the country. Realty Connect USA has 17 offices in Nassau, Suffolk, and Queens Counties in New York with over 700 Real Estate Agents.

**https://longislandprobateresource.com/**
**https://www.facebook.com/LIProbateResource/**
**https://www.linkedin.com/in/peter-demidovich-173516118/**
**Email: Peter@PeterDemidovich.com**
**Phone: 516-983-5109**

# The Use of Home Equity in Retirement
## By Sue Haviland

**Question:**

IS THERE A WAY to use your home equity to help you financially during retirement?

**Answer:**

I've been privileged to spend over 20 years in the reverse mortgage space as an originator, trainer, speaker, author, and coach. I have engaged in conversation with many, many older adults and their families over the years who express various reasons for considering utilizing home equity in retirement. The reverse mortgage programs of today have significant safeguards built into the program, making them a particularly good option for older adult homeowners. It's easy to say, "I'll simply take out a reverse mortgage and remain in my home," as if merely having the available funds will address any issues. For many, that is the best course of action. Consider, however, the following story:

"My parents started the reverse mortgage process and invited me to the initial meeting with the loan officer to review the paperwork. It had been a while since I'd been to visit and had no idea my father's situation had deteriorated. He has significant mobility issues and refuses to walk with a cane or walker. He grips the handrail and walks very unsteadily down the stairs. It is evident he is no longer safe in this 3-story townhome. Is it worth the time, effort, and money to modify the house using reverse mortgage funds? Or is it better to sell the home and move?"

Faced with this scenario, the conversation will shift from its original focus. It's obvious that remaining in the current home without significant modification is not the best option for this husband and wife. And how would those modifications look? The husband would need ongoing assistance navigating the house, potentially creating an unsafe situation. Couple that with the fact that if he were to experience a fall, would his wife be able to assist him without putting herself at risk?

The theme of this book is "Difficult Conversations." A conversation about reverse mortgage options may be considered difficult by some, but it doesn't have to be that way. As with any important financial decision, the variables, features, and a clear understanding of how the decision will impact the individual must be considered.

Let's take a step back and consider all that the reverse mortgage program can accomplish for older adult homeowners. Often regarded in the past as a loan of last resort, today's reverse mortgage borrower realizes the power of utilizing home equity as one approaches retirement. The definition of a reverse mortgage is straightforward—it allows an older adult homeowner to convert a portion of their primary residence's equity into cash. Since FHA first began insuring reverse mortgages in 1989, under the Reagan administration, over 1.3 million borrowers have taken advantage of this unique product (see the attachment at the end of this chapter to learn more). A reverse mortgage can mean financial freedom and a choice of options for older adult homeowners. The many safeguards built into the program provide a comfort level to both the borrowers and adult children, who of course, want what's best for mom and dad. Indeed, it's often the adult children who make the first inquiry and start the reverse mortgage conversation. As in the story at the beginning of this section, the adult son was quite involved in the discussion. The safeguards built into today's reverse mortgages include:

**Non-recourse feature:** Should the borrower pass away or sell the home, neither the borrower nor the heirs will owe more than the home is worth. Plainly stated, if the home is "upside down," the borrower or heirs are not responsible for the deficit.

**Non-Borrowing Spouse Protections:** In the case of the FHA Home Equity Conversion Mortgage (HECM), should a borrower pre-decease an eligible non-borrowing spouse, that spouse may have certain protections under the program. This offers peace of mind in cases where one spouse has not yet reached the minimum age of 62 when the loan is taken out.

**Required Counseling:** All borrowers, non-borrowing spouses, and others noted on the deed are required to participate in a counseling session which is conducted by a HUD approved agency. This session allows the borrowers to ask questions of the counselor before deciding to move forward with the reverse mortgage application. Once the session is completed, the borrower(s) receives a certificate which is presented to the lender. This certificate is generally good for 180 days, allowing the prospective borrower to take his/her time or consult with family or trusted advisors.

The FHA insured reverse mortgage, or HECM is the most popular reverse mortgage and is available nationwide. The product is closely monitored to protect the best interests of the older adult borrower and the longevity of the program. It enjoys a high approval rating. Indeed many borrowers are pleased with their decision to utilize a reverse mortgage as part of an overall retirement planning strategy.

One of the many features of a HECM reverse mortgage is the variety of options for accessing the proceeds of the loan. Borrowers may opt for a fixed rate HECM, which as the name implies, carries an interest rate that remains fixed for the life of the loan. It allows for a one-time lump sum disbursement and can be best suitable for a borrower who has a current mortgage balance close to the amount of the available proceeds (any outstanding mortgage must be paid either prior to or at the closing of a reverse mortgage) or has some other immediate use for the funds.

An adjustable rate HECM allows for flexible payout options, including:

- Monthly amounts either for a set term (ex: 10 years) or tenure—meaning for the entire life of the loan.
- A line of credit option. The line of credit within a HECM is like a traditional line of credit in that the borrower can access funds in any amount for any purpose such as modifying the home to meet the borrower's needs, both today and tomorrow. This was the question posed by the adult child in our example above. Is the best option to utilize the funds from a reverse mortgage to make these needed changes to the home? There are, however, a couple of important distinctions. One is the growth feature built into the HECM line of credit. Yes, that's right. The unused portion of the line of credit increases over time, providing increased borrowing power. This feature showcases the power of the HECM line of credit as part of an overall retirement plan. Funds are available as needed to cover unforeseen expenditures or home modifications, for example. The line of credit also allows the borrower to make payments and then access the funds again.
- The above options can be combined to meet the needs and goals of the borrower. In addition, the borrower can alter the payment plan for any remaining funds by contacting the servicer.

In addition to the HECM option, there are proprietary reverse mortgage products available in the marketplace today. These are administered by the lenders who offer them, but often are attractive to borrowers who have higher value homes or situations that fall outside of typical HECM guidelines. An experienced reverse mortgage consultant can offer guidance on the best product option for a borrower.

A discussion on reverse mortgages would not be complete without examining when the loan becomes due and payable. Unlike a conventional mortgage which typically carries a fixed term of 15, 20, 30 years, a reverse mortgage's term is determined by the borrower. As long as at least one borrower continues to live in the home as the primary residence and uphold the other requirements of the loan (keeping property charges including real estate taxes, hazard and flood insurance, HOA, or condo fees current at all times and keeping the home in good repair) the loan remains in place. When the last remaining borrower permanently moves from the home (passes away or sells the property) the loan is due.

The reasons for utilizing a reverse mortgage as part of an overall retirement plan are as many and varied as the borrowers themselves. Some borrowers simply want to supplement their monthly cash flow. Some look to "retire" that monthly mortgage payment. Others seek to establish a line of credit and the growth feature it includes to plan for the future. This can provide that all important safety net and peace of mind that unexpected expenses won't break the bank. Other reasons include travel, a college fund for the grandchildren, modifications to the home which allow the borrower to safely age in place, even utilizing reverse mortgage proceeds to purchase a vacation or investment property.

Still others put a reverse mortgage to work when purchasing a new primary residence. Yes, you read that right! A reverse mortgage can be used in the purchase of a home—what an interesting solution for an older adult looking to identify the perfect home for aging in place. Let's look back at the story from the beginning of this section. The father had significant difficulty navigating the stairs in a 3-level home. The adult children have expressed concern, and no one is sure what the solution should be. In this situation, a good option for these clients is a reverse for purchase. This will satisfy their desire to remain homeowners and allow them to select a one level home closer to their adult children (remember the son admitted that he had not visited his parents recently). While they are considering available homes, speaking with a real estate professional who specializes in working with older adults, they may make a list of other aging in place related features their new home should have: zero threshold entry way, lever door handles, maintenance-free exterior, etc. They will also have peace of mind knowing that they can make this goal a reality without the burden of a mandatory mortgage payment each month.

As with any financial decision, the potential borrower should make certain that the product will meet their goals and needs. A reverse mortgage is not a band-aid. It's not meant to be a short-term fix. The loan is intended for those borrowers who intend to remain in the home for the longer term (of course none of us knows what the future holds). If the older adult plans to move in the near future or if the home itself doesn't meet the borrower's physical needs, another option should be considered (as in our example in which the couple decides to purchase a home using a reverse mortgage vs. using the product to remain in the current property). Family members or other trusted advisors may be included in the discussion to be sure all questions are answered, and the best possible decision is reached. An experienced reverse mortgage professional should be consulted to address all questions and ensure that the consideration of a reverse mortgage isn't a difficult conversation.

This booklet provided by the National Council on Aging, provides valuable information for anyone considering a reverse mortgage.

Find it here:

A Guide to Use Your Home to Stay at Home (ncoa.org)

The National Reverse Mortgage Lenders Association is the national voice of the reverse mortgage industry. NRMLA Members must adhere to a strict **Code of Ethics & Professional Responsibility** that requires the highest ethical treatment of reverse mortgage customers before, during, and after they receive their loans.

\* Source: HUD (Through May 2023)

## Sue Haviland, CRMP

SUE HAVILAND HAS BEEN a leader in the reverse mortgage industry for over 20 years. She has been an originator, trainer, speaker, author, and host of the radio show "Senior Spotlight with Sue Haviland" covering a wide variety of topics of interest to older adults. She has been a featured speaker at numerous industry events and has a passion for helping others succeed. Sue is a Certified Reverse Mortgage Professional (CRMP), and NAIPC Board Member, ATD Master Trainer, and holds the CAPS (Certified Aging In Place) certification.

Sue is president and CEO of Step Smart, a southwest Florida-based nonprofit educating the public on fall prevention, its risk factors, and actions to make a safer home. She is a proud member of the Marco Island Noontime Rotary and a graduate of the Rotary Leadership Institute. You will often find Sue volunteering at a Rotary event both locally and in the district.

She and her husband, Wayne reside in Marco Island, Florida. They have 2 children and 4 very active grandchildren.

# Aging Solo

## By Carolyn Novotny

**Question:**

MY HUSBAND AND I are "aging solo." What does that mean? And how can we best prepare for later in life?

**Answer:**

We have no extended family to help us as we age, except for each other. One person usually goes first so that would make the other person "age solo." That, in itself, can be a scary proposition. What makes our situation even more stressful is I am the caregiver for my elderly mother, and I am planning for her needs also.

Some people might say, "What is the big deal? Just contact an attorney and draw up a Trust." Sounds simple, but it is not. How do you communicate your wishes to others so that your Trust can be properly executed? Remember, we have no extended family. Who do you make your Trustee? Who do you share your plans with? How do you start that conversation with yourself and others? This is where things get difficult. It is hard enough to have these types of conversations with your parents or your family. How do you have this conversation with a good friend?

You need to think about who you can trust with intimate information about your life. I have heard that privacy is defined by "what others do not know about you." Giving up your privacy is difficult. You are sharing your plans, your finances, your desires for your medical care or end-of-life. Will they be willing to take on the responsibility? Can you depend on them? Will they be willing to take on the extra caregiving responsibility of my mother? If not, how are we handling that? Remember your Trustee is not just for handling things after you die. They could also get involved if you become incapacitated. Trust works while you are alive as well as after your death. Also, think about their age. You want them to outlive you. All of this can be overwhelming. Yet, doing nothing can be devastating.

After you have decided who might fit this profile as your "trusted friend," (some people call them your "chosen family"), how are you planning on approaching them? They will be acting as your fiduciary. First you need to do your homework. You need to fully understand what you are asking a friend to do. Be honest with yourself and with your friend. Do not leave out anything. There is a form called "Five Wishes." A good starting place to find this form is www.fivewishes.org. Other places will also come up if you type Five Wishes in the Internet search bar. It could help you organize your thoughts. Proper planning and communication can help remove extra work for your friend. Remember they are doing you a favor.

They will need access to your home. You will need to put your information in a place they can find it and keep this information up to date. This includes information to access your attorney who is handling your Trust.

Don't forget your pets in your planning. They are family, too. This information is usually not part of your Trust, but just as important. Who is their veterinarian? What do they eat? I am not aware of an Advanced Health Directive for animals. Your veterinarian needs to be aware of your Trustee, whether they are a trusted friend or a professional fiduciary. Without your approval a lot of veterinarians will not talk to your Trustee, provide information about your pet or, in some cases, even treat your pet. This varies from state to state and needs to be taken into consideration. Your wishes for your pet need to be part of your plan. If you want someone to adopt your pet, make sure that they are willing to do so.

Now that you have determined the friend you feel you can trust to fulfill your wishes, how do you approach them? First you will need to have all of the information at your fingertips to explain why you are reaching out to them and the importance of choosing them. You do not want them to feel that they need to say yes or no immediately. Give them time, but not too much time, to think about what you are asking of them. Show them that you are prepared with:

- Your Trust
- An attorney
- A CPA
- If you want to stay in your home, share your plans. Your friend should realize that you are not asking them to take care of you.
- If you need to move out, what does that look like?
- Plans for any family member that you are responsible for
- Plans for your pet that probably should show that you are not asking your friend to take care of them.
- Preplanned burial. If possible, you should make the arrangements and pay for it.
- It would be great to include your friend in the planning process, if possible. That is your choice.

o   Make sure that your Trustee knows who your team are.

Now that you have your first "Trusted Friend" you should think about finding a second one. When you set up any Trust, your Trustees should be two deep in the event something happens to your first pick. You can also use a Professional Fiduciary/Trustee in either the first or second position. A lot of people are more comfortable doing this as they do not want to give up their "privacy" to a friend, and that is understandable.

If you choose to use a Professional Fiduciary/Trustee, the basic planning is the same, however, you also need to take additional steps in picking that person. Different people can act as a Fiduciary. As we said earlier, your "Trusted Friend" will be acting as a Fiduciary. However, if you are looking to hire a Professional Fiduciary you want to make sure that they are licensed. Your banker or Investment Advisor could act as your Fiduciary. However, they are not required to be licensed. You need to understand the meaning of a Fiduciary. Moral and ethical issues need to be considered and that there are no conflicts of interest. As with a Trusted Friend, you also need to think about their age. You want them to outlive you. The book, *Ethics for Trustees 2.0: A Guide for All Who Serve as Trustee*, by Marqueite C. Larenz, might be helpful.

In California you can find information on Fiduciaries and their training and licensing at www.fiduciary.ca.gov. I am sure that other states have similar sites. Another source is Independent Trust Alliance, www.trusteealliance.com. Do your homework.

We cannot forget that we need to plan for my mother also. She has early stages of dementia. It is difficult for families to deal with this. Now you are also asking your Trusted Friend to deal with the situation. If you are in this situation, you might want to look at some type of Conservatorship to be able to plan for now and for the future. This could include hiring a Supportive Decision Maker. This is usually not just one person, but several in different areas such as a financial decision maker, medical decision person etc. These different people all need to work together. Even though my mother has cognitive issues we want to make sure that her wishes are taken into consideration. I know my mother. However, it is not fair to expect our Trusted Friend to take on this responsibility also. This is where Supportive Decision Makers come in. You need to be clear in your planning as to how your loved one is engaged and what changes in the decision-making process they are involved in. What changes in their mental capacity changes their involvement? This can be complex and should not be taken lightly.

You need to communicate with others who your "Trusted Friend" and/or the Professional Fiduciary is so they know who to contact if something happens to you. This means notifying your neighbor, someone you have coffee regularly with, or people you see on a regular basis. Give them something with the information on your Trusted Friend or Professional Fiduciary and tell them, "I am sure that you know that I do not have any immediate family, however I want you to know that my good friend (put in the name of your trusted friend or professional) has agreed to help me. Here is their information in case something happens to me."

Also, keep that information in your wallet, car, phone, or any place people would logically look. Follow up with your Trusted Friend or professional fiduciary on a regular basis. Things change. Their situation could change, and they will no longer be able to help you. This is why we recommend that your Trustee is two deep, and you are also thinking about what is next.

If you are blessed to have family that you can trust and depend on, you should handle your wishes with them in the same manner as you handle a Trusted Friend. Do not let your trust sit on a shelf and collect dust. Some suggest that you review your Trust every year. Others suggest that you should review it every two years.

What prompted my husband and I to realize we had not taken care of our planning, including the planning to make sure my mother was taken care of, was a friend that was Aging Solo and had a serious vehicle accident. None of his friends knew anything about his wishes. None of his friends had access to his home to see if he had a Trust and who could make medical decisions for him because he was in a coma. When we realized that he was not going to make it, none of us knew his final wishes. One of his friends had some experience in this area and with a lot of time and luck was able to find a way to enter his home legally and find some information. We are all sure that as much as we tried, none of us truly knew his wishes. As his friends we did the best we could. Our friend's estate is now going through probate. The state is making the decisions. If any good can come out of this situation we all realized that we needed to be better friends. Several of us are "Aging Solo," and we are now having "The Conversation" with each other. We are all willing to help each other because we know the outcome if you do not. In a strange way, his accident has made it easier for any of us to have The Conversations. We are the lucky ones.

People are sometimes afraid that if they plan, they will die. We can all become incapacitated or die. Not planning not only hurts you, also the people that love and care about you, friends, or family.

PLAN
COMMUNICATE
TRUST OTHERS
BE A GOOD FRIEND TO OTHERS AND YOURSELF
LIVE YOUR BEST LIFE

In reality, we should all plan as if we are "Aging Solo" because at some point we might be.

If you would like to share any of your experiences about "Aging Solo" I would love to hear from you. We are all in this together.

## Carolyn Novotny

I EARNED MY WINGS in the Senior Industry by starting the journey being my Mother's Caregiver. After spending over 35 years as a Commercial Insurance Broker I started Access 2 Senior Living to help people in transition thrive in their environment and to remove Stress from the Seniors and their Loved Ones. Knowledge is the key. Planning is a must. There must be a buy in by everyone involved including the Senior, their Loved Ones, their Financial Planner, their CPA (Tax Person) their Trustee (Fiduciary). I am a current member of National Aging in Place Council and past Chair of the Orange County Chapter in California.

There are no easy answers, just good solutions.

**LinkedIn:**

www.linkedin.com/in/Carolyn-Novotny-Access2seniorliving

**Business website:**

www.access2seniorliving.com

# TRANSPORTATION & TRAVEL

# When Is It Time to Take Away the Keys?
## By Melanie Henry

**Question:**

Did you know adult children would rather talk to their parents about funeral plans than talk about driving concerns?[14] No one wants to be the "bad guy" and take the keys away too early. But how do you know if your parent is still safe to drive? Who is the best person to bring this topic up, and how do you have "the talk" while saving your relationship and sanity?

**Answer:**

For most people living in the US, driving represents the ultimate symbol of having complete independence and freedom. It's all about having that sense of being in charge of your own life. But as we get older, the whole idea of control becomes even more important, and it can bring on some serious anxiety and fear for some. Losing control over anything that represents freedom and independence can really hit a nerve and become a touchy subject. For most of us, driving is one part of life that we really don't want to lose control over. It's right up there on the list of stuff we hold onto tightly.

Many families find this subject challenging to talk about. Families can be hesitant to bring up the topic of driving, knowing they will be

---

14 National Safety Council and Caring.com nationwide survey of baby boomers, 2008.

faced with resistance, denial, or even hostility. Threats to disinherit adult children and severing relationships can lead to fear and a real reluctance of adult children wanting to be involved.

It's frustrating and worrying when a parent does not share the same concerns and do not seem to notice or care about the potential dangers. Families don't want to upset their loved one and worry they will get depressed, angry, and upset with them.

Most older adults have more experience than other drivers, and many feel they are entitled to drive because of their years of experience. It is a common response for aging drivers to downplay concerns, avoid the topic, or deny there's even an issue.

There exists a myth about driving. When you hear your parent say, "I'm fine. I'm safe. I only drive a couple of miles to the store." This is a myth. Regardless of how many miles, an unsafe older driver has the same level of risk regardless of 1 mile or 10 miles.

Now add to this mix a parent or spouse with a cognitive impairment and this issue just became even more amplified. No wonder talking about driving concerns is a conversation many families dread having!

There are some individuals who believe that driving is a right, when it should be viewed as a privilege that comes with great responsibility. We all need to recognize our own limitations and be aware of everything we can do to be safe on the road. Our safety and lives depend on each other to be fully aware and mentally engaged behind the wheel.

Research shows that as a group, older drivers are typically safe. The actual number of accidents involving older drivers decreases as age increases.[15] Experts attribute this decline to self-imposed restrictions, such as driving less miles, not driving at night, avoiding rush-hour traffic, and reduced freeway driving. Enhanced safety features on vehicles are likely contributing to lower crash collision rates as well.

---

15  The Hartford|MIT Age Lab, We Need To Talk...Family Conversations with Older Drivers.

By the year 2030, one of every five drivers in America will be 65 years of age or older, estimated to be some 44 million drivers.[16] According to the US Census Bureau, the population 70 and older is projected to increase to 53 million in 2030.[17] Drivers aged 70 plus drive fewer miles but are keeping their licenses for longer.[18]

However, older drivers, especially after age 75, have a higher risk of being involved in a collision for every mile they drive. The rate of risk is nearly equal to the risk of younger drivers aged 16 to 24. The rate of fatalities increases slightly after age 65 and significantly after age 75. This increased fatal crash rate is due to the increased susceptibility to injury, particularly chest injuries, and medical complications, rather than an increased tendency to get into crashes.[19]

The American Medical Association (AMA) estimates that the per-mile fatality rate for drivers over 85 years old is nine times as great as drivers 25 to 69 years old. The most at-risk driver is the one with cognitive impairment. Drivers with a cognitive impairment are more than three times as likely to cause an at-fault collision.[20] The Alzheimer's Association predicts that 1 in 9 baby boomers are at risk of cognitive impairment and the risk increases with age.[21]

There are over 5.8 million Americans living with dementia, and it is estimated that 30-40% still drive.[22] That means that 1,740,000 to 2,320,000 individuals are driving with dementia in the United States.

---

16  The Hartford|MIT Age Lab, We Need To Talk...Family Conversations with Older Drivers and Insurance.
17  US Census Bureau, 2017.
18  Insurance Institute on Highway Safety (iihs.org), Older People - A summary of fatality statistics about older people compiled by IIHS from 2021 Fatality Analysis Reporting.
19  Cicchino, J. B. (2015). Why have fatality rates among older drivers declined? The relative contributions of changes in survivability and crash involvement. Accident Analysis and Prevention, 83, 67-73. Insurance Institute on Highway Safety (iihs.org), Older People - A summary of fatality statistics about older people compiled by IIHS from 2021 Fatality Analysis Reporting.
20  DriveABLE Impirica Impairment Assessment Technologies, Alberta, Canada.
21  https://www.alz.org
22  https://www.alz.org

It is normal that older adults want to drive. They like the independence, and most want to "age in place" by living in their own home, maintain a certain lifestyle, keep their identity and sense of self. The problem is that the people who are driving with dementia often have no clue that they are unsafe to drive and do not typically retire from driving without intervention from family or medical professionals.

According to data from the Insurance Institute on Highway Safety (IHSS), a total of 5,209 people ages 70 and older died in crashes in 2021. In 2020, motor vehicle crashes accounted for less than 1 percent of fatalities among people 70 and older. Although older drivers with health issues may be safe drivers, they have a higher risk of injury or death in an accident, regardless of who is at fault.[23]

According to the Storefront Safety Council, there are more than 100 vehicles crashing into storefronts every single day in this country. Each year in the US, as many as 16,000 people are injured and as many as 2,600 are killed in vehicle-into-building crashes. The most frequent causes are operator error (21%) and pedal error (20%).[24]

Just because a person is getting older does not make them an unsafe driver. Some people age will age gracefully and drive safely until the very end. Thankfully, there is a large group of drivers who choose to give up driving on their own, without being asked. Those drivers should be publicly recognized and awarded a medal for driver retirement!

It is the driver aged 80 and above who is at greater risk of being injured or killed in a collision, regardless of fault.[25] And if the person has a cognitive impairment, the risk escalates significantly.

---

[23] DriveABLE Impirica & Insurance Institute on Highway Safety (iihs.org), Older People - A summary of fatality statistics about older people compiled by IIHS from 2021 Fatality Analysis Reporting.
[24] StorefrontSafety.org
[25] DriveABLE Impirica & Insurance Institute on Highway Safety (iihs.org), Older People - A summary of fatality statistics about older people compiled by IIHS from 2021 Fatality Analysis Reporting.

## When Is It Time to Take Away the Keys?

The number one takeaway I share with families is to try and put yourself in the shoes of your mom or dad. Giving up the keys can be devastating news and, for most drivers, is a life changing event. Research shows that the following six months post-driving is a critical period. Older adults who are required to stop driving are at high risk of depression and social isolation if alternate transportation options are not in place and support systems are lacking.

Your role and support as an adult child are imperative to your parent's driving safety. It takes courage, sensitivity, strength, and love to navigate through this worrying time as you figure out if your loved one is still safe to drive. Families have an important role in helping the older driver make safe driving decisions and ensure peace of mind for the entire family. As hard it might be, families have to take responsibility because your loved one may no longer be able to do this for themselves.

There are many warning signs that there may be a problem.

**Warning Signs**

The driving behaviors listed below could cause safety problems. Since driving ability seldom changes drastically in a short time, you should be able to track changes over time to get a clear picture of overall driving ability.

Here's how to use this list.

- Observe driving over time, keeping notes to help you understand **changes** in driving ability.
- Look for a **pattern** of warning signs and for an increase in the frequency of occurrence.

**Warning Signs:**

- Unaware of driving errors, belief they are still a good safe driver, lack of insight and awareness

- Unaware of other vehicles, cyclists, and pedestrians
- Difficulty turning head to see when backing up
- Failing to use side mirrors
- Close calls / near misses
- Riding the brake
- Confusing the brake and gas pedals
- Easily distracted while driving
- Being honked at by other drivers
- Incorrect signaling
- Parking inappropriately
- Hitting curbs
- Trouble navigating turns
- Scrapes or dents on the car, mailbox, or garage
- Increased agitation or irritation when driving
- Declining confidence when driving
- Failure to notice important activity on the side of the road
- Failure to stop at stop sign or red light
- Poor judgment with left turns
- Failure to notice traffic signs
- Moves into wrong lane
- Difficulty maintaining lane position
- Not anticipating potentially dangerous situations
- Driving too slowly (typically) or too fast
- Uses a "co-pilot"
- Delayed response to unexpected situations
- Parking incorrectly and confusion at parking lot exits
- Getting lost driving to and from store
- Forgetting purpose of trips
- Disorientation in familiar places
- Ticketed moving violations or warnings

- Collision
- Stopping in traffic for no apparent reason
- Friends no longer wanting to ride with you or your loved one

Other non-driving warnings signs include:
- Decline in ability to do everyday tasks
- Confusion with taking medications correctly
- Two or more falls in a year
- Loss of strength or balance
- Changes in physical status
- Mild cognitive impairment may indicate a cognitive driving assessment is necessary.

As a family you will need to decide who is the best person to be talking with your loved one. Often it is the adult child closest to the parent.

Ask yourself: Would I allow my grandchild or child to ride alone with my spouse/mom/dad?

If you are unsure, then see for yourself and go for a ride-along. If you have reason to believe there may be a problem, please do not take their word for it as your parent may honestly believe all is fine and well with their driving.

Ideally, ride-alongs should be planned before you have driving concerns. It will help minimize stress and anxiety for your parent If this becomes a normal part of your visit and time together. That way you can keep track and look for any changes or patterns that may be occurring. Using a checklist will help give you a baseline to systematically evaluate driving performance.

If your loved one is refusing to allow you to ride-along and is suspicious of your motives, believing you are trying to take away the car keys, then you can always suggest an independent, objective driving assessment and "prove you wrong." Sometimes this can be a motivating factor.

Driver Rehabilitation Specialists (DRS) are qualified to conduct these types of assessments. If you live in the San Francisco Bay Area, my service, the Driver Cognitive Assessment Center (DCAC) provides an objective cognitive driving assessment that will provide you with fair and accurate information about driver risk and safety. Please contact our office if you would like contact information for a local DRS or more information about our services.

If possible, ride-along several times at different times of the day. Have your loved one drive to their normal destinations. If you do not see any warning signs, then repeat the ride-along every few months. The reality is we all decline in one way or another as we age. The physical and mental abilities we need to be good safe drivers may also decline.

It is estimated that over ninety percent of what we process when driving is through our eyes.[26] A comprehensive yearly vision exam is essential to rule out eye diseases such as cataracts, macular degeneration, glaucoma, and other eye conditions that may impair driving abilities.

If your parent is not doing well on the ride-along, do not address this while you are in the car together. Swap driving positions if you are truly scared and get home safely. Remain calm and say as kindly as possible that after driving with them today, you are worried and think it is time for a checkup with the doctor to make sure everything is okay.

If your loved one lives in the San Francisco Bay Area and does not want to talk about this with their doctor, preferring to keep this a private family matter, the process and technology offered at the DCAC may be more suitable (Driver Cognitive Assessment Center, LLC (DCAC) Ph 925.249.5947 www.dcacbayarea.com). In the San Francisco Bay Area, drivers and families may contact our service directly and no physician referral is required. This technology is also available in other states but

---

[26] ADED – Association Driver Rehabilitation Specialists – The Impact of Disability, Vision, and Aging on Driving, 2022.

through a hospital setting Please contact our office if you need assistance with locating a provider. We are more than happy to help connect you.

There will be some families who will have to deal with a difficult parent who is refusing to cooperate at every level and is in complete denial there is anything to be concerned about driving-wise.

You have a number of options to safeguard your loved one. Some families will hide the car keys, disable the car battery, move the vehicle off the property, or grind down the car key. While it provides an immediate but sometimes temporary resolution to the driving issue, it can also create intense anger, hostility, and resentment from your loved one. Relationships can be permanently damaged and trust eroded between a parent and adult child.

If you meet resistance from your loved one to have a checkup with their doctor, or refusal to participate in a driving assessment, you can and should write a letter to your parent's physician asking for their help. Describe as accurately and succinctly as possible your observations and share your safety concerns.

The timing of when to bring up the subject of driving is important. If there has been a change in physical status such as a fall, an illness, hospitalization, urgent care visit, changes in medical condition, starting a new medication or any event that can impact mental abilities and alertness is a critical time to talk about driving concerns and safety.

For many people, there is no single incident that occurs. There may be a general gradual decline in physical strength, balance, alertness, concentration levels, reaction times, memory, and a declining ability to take care of themselves. Some drivers will limit their own driving without being asked. Others will need family to guide the conversation and restrictions needed.

Limited driving may mean, no longer driving at night, or in peak-hours. It may include driving shorter distances so there is less fatigue and for others no freeway driving. It may include no longer driving to unfamiliar places or driving in poor weather conditions.

Family conversations do make a difference. What you say or don't say influences the decisions of your loved one and can make the difference between staying safe or being at risk or worse. Although these conversations can be uncomfortable, they can help your loved one to make decisions that are in the best interests of their own safety.

Be prepared to have several conversations with your loved one. A calm response will help to diffuse negative emotions. Some family members will have strong emotions ranging from anger and frustration, while others may feel guilty. And some family members may not believe there is a driving issue. In reaching the goal of ensuring your parent remains safe, it is important that adult children present a united front. In situations where family dynamics are challenging, think about engaging the help of a geriatric care manager or aged life care professional who is qualified in mediation and conflict resolution.

You will have a more positive outcome if you involve your loved one in the conversation versus telling them how it will be. Consider the personalities involved and past experience of family members talking about difficult issues. Some families mistakenly delegate the most outspoken or authoritative person to speak. Often it is best for this person to have the role of enforcing the driving decisions.

It is imperative for those family members involved to work together with your loved one about the agreements limiting driving. The reality is that limited driving signifies that changes are starting to occur and family members and possibly friends will need to be proactive in ongoing observation of driving skills.

When a discussion about driving is necessary, be prepared, be strategic, and open the discussion.

## Be Prepared.

Make a list of safety and medical concerns.
> Explore legal concerns and licensing requirements.
> Plan early, especially if illness is progressive, finances, and health.
> Research future transportation needs and resources available.

## Be Strategic.

Consider family dynamics, some family members may not acknowledge the problem.
> Decide who would be best to raise the topic and have a conversation.

Be aware that the driver may lack insight and awareness of any driving problem.
> Expect resistance, find out what driving means to the person.
> Remain positive, focus on what you can do.
> Be sensitive but resolved.

## Open the Discussion.

When appropriate, acknowledge the driver's past driving record and experience.
> Note that things have changed.
> Blame the medical condition, not the person.
> Discuss the implications of having a crash.
> Be responsive to concerns.
> Focus on the need for a driving assessment.

Talk about alternate transportation options.

Contact a family mediation professional, geriatric care manager, or aged life care professional to help mediate if there is conflict and ongoing tension.

## Melanie Henry

MELANIE HENRY is the founder and CEO of the Driver Cognitive Assessment Center, LLC (DCAC). Arriving in the US from Australia in 2007, Melanie experienced many adjustments including driving on the "right" side of the road. It was during her time as Transportation Coordinator for a volunteer driver medical ride program for seniors that she recognized the need for an independent and objective driver cognitive assessment service. Melanie's professional career spans decades working in the field of social welfare, risk assessment, and case management in the child protection and criminal child abuse investigations arena. She has been a privately employed caregiver and is a licensed driving school instructor.

Melanie is currently pursuing her certification in the Driver Rehabilitation Professional field to better assist drivers with mobility needs. She is an active member of organizations such as Association Driver Rehabilitation Specialists (ADED), National Mobility Equipment

Dealers Association (NMEDA), and is currently serving as Secretary for the National Aging in Place Council, San Francisco Bay Area Chapter, bringing professionals and communities together supporting aging in place through collaboration, education, and advocacy.

# What If You DIE When Traveling? Face the Unthinkable and Avoid Crisis Mode

By Helen Scherrer-Diamond

**Question:**

I LOVE TO TRAVEL and want to continue as long as possible. Though my partner and I are healthy, I am a little concerned about what would happen if we passed away while traveling in a foreign country or on a cruise ship. Is there anything we can do to plan in advance for this? If anything happens, I don't want my children to have to worry about this sort of thing in addition to grieving and making funeral arrangements.

**Answer:**

Yes, you can apply to my Inman Travel Plan Coverage for a one-time lifetime fee per person. If you travel 75 miles or more away from your legal place of residence, Inman Travel Plan handles all needed procedures. Let me tell you how and why!

Traveling internationally or domestically can be challenging, even if you have the best intentions and you plan ahead of time with funeral arrangements. If you or your travel partner dies while traveling, the issues are many. For example, you may not speak the language. You may not know where the nearest funeral home is, and you may be "taken advantage of" in not knowing efficient mileage and affordable costs. You may not know if the death certificate can be issued quickly and where your body will be stored. You may not understand embalming vs. refrigeration. You may not know the proper procedures or plans about how to have a body brought home to the legal state of residence and if the procedures can be handled correctly and quickly.

At death, when traveling, the "procedures" in handling "the deceased" are very important for legal reasons. Yes, people can "plan in advance" and pay for travel plan coverage (in case of death) ahead of time. A global company like Inman Travel Plan is experienced in all of these important procedures to help the traveling partner or family members left behind with what to do. Repatriation and state laws can be scary to face alone.

As an example of "crisis mode," I would like to share two stories about death when traveling. A family recently had to bring back their family member/loved one, a 61-year-old man, from Thailand. The man was hiking in the mountains near a cave and fell to his untimely death. The family was obviously devastated! They had no idea where to begin the process nor really what to do to "handle his body." They relied on a lot of the arrangements which were dependent upon local help in Thailand. From information shared, repatriation cost the family $16,000 to bring his body back to Australia.

Another family, a husband and wife, using our funeral home in Chamblee, GA, lived in Sandy Springs, GA. While cruising at retirement on a ship in Italy, the husband had a heart attack and died unexpectedly. While the wife was devasted and in shock, she still had to figure out how, with the help of the Captain of the ship, to bring her husband's body back to the USA. The husband had a heart attack and the wife needed to grieve, not worry about procedures and a timely burial at home. It cost the wife and family $11,000 to bring him back to Georgia!

Planning ahead of time to avoid crisis mode and face the unthinkable like a death away from home, means doing your due diligence and knowing your options ahead of time. As a licensed Insurance Agent in

## WHAT IF YOU DIE WHEN TRAVELING?

Life and Health, I help individuals and couples with the pre-planning of their own funeral arrangements, and I highly recommend having the Inman Travel Plan coverage, too, in case of DEATH. Most travel insurance offered by travel agents, airlines, and insurance carriers, covers ILLNESS or INJURY, not DEATH. Most travel insurance for illness or injury is paid at each travel trip. With the Inman Travel Plan coverage, the cost is a one-time, lifetime fee. And most travel insurance carriers may not even know exact procedures. They just offer reimbursement for costs. Dealing with Medical Teams, Consulates, Embassies, Passports, and Customs can be frightening. And it can be expensive to hire an emergency helicopter or other transport vehicle, too.

Wake up Travelers! Breaking your neck on a hiking trail in another country or another state can happen. Falling off a zip-line can happen. Skiing into a tree and breaking your neck can happen. Would you or your travel partner know what to do?

Wake up Snowbirds! Dying from a heart attack on a cruise ship (as you read earlier in my chapter) can happen. Or think about if your spouse died at your second residence, a vacation home. Would you know what to do?

Seniors look forward to traveling upon retirement. Seniors who travel to another state in the United States or Internationally to another country can avoid crisis mode! Protect yourselves and have the Inman Travel (Protection) Plan coverage just because of your age! Not to SCARE but to prepare, and just BE AWARE that the procedures, when you are traveling domestically or internationally, need to be handled and are most important. Ignorance is NOT bliss, and it can be costly!

The costs at death when traveling, like repatriation from another country, can be very expensive for a number of reasons. Consulates and Embassies and Immigration and Passports can become an issue. Issues like being on a cruise ship in the wrong port of call, can happen. Not knowing the foreign language to discuss the procedures at the port of call has happened, even with the expertise of the Captain on a cruise ship. Think about it. What if the ship has to dock in the port of call in another country to transport the deceased? Sometimes even a helicopter and the closest heliport to transport the body may be needed and cause havoc. Lack of knowledge of procedures is costly and can be very untimely.

As travelers, you need to recognize that if your body needed to be brought back to your legal state of residence from a cruise ship, from another country. or even from another US state, laws are different. Everyone needs to recognize that a deceased body has to have the declaration of the exact cause of death on the death certificate by a certified medical person or recognized clinician. Everyone needs to recognize that the deceased body needs to be embalmed OR refrigerated until transportation can be obtained. Everyone needs to understand that a container like a casket to transport a body must be handled legally and be obtained. Everyone who travels needs to understand that the mode of transportation (ship, train, airline, or hearse) to transport a body back to the legal state of residence, must be obtained and approved for cargo of the deceased body, and that a funeral director is always involved. The death certificate must be legally obtained, too.

When traveling, if you die, please know too that you can be buried or cremated in that country or US state to which you traveled to and died in. However, arrangements and payment still need to be made, and those decisions should be YOURS ahead of time! Your loved ones and travel partners need to grieve, not make financial and emotional decisions under stress for you.

As a Licensed Agent and Community Outreach Director, I am always asked, "Can I plan my own funeral ahead of time?" and the answer is a very loud and passionate, "YES, PLEASE DO!" That way, you can help avoid the emotional and financial decision-making and the stress

## What If You Die When Traveling?

you cause for your travel partner and/or loved ones who need to make your decisions on your behalf. Having pre-planned funeral arrangements in writing is *so important*. Coverage by Inman Travel Plan is separate and most important, too! Hopefully your arrangements are also paid for ahead of time with your local funeral home, in your legal state of residence. You can also pre-plan with a funeral home in another state or country, but *please* know that it is your local funeral director who may need to help with coordination of all the arrangements you made because of your legal state of residence. And your death certificate and notification to the Social Security Administration is based on your legal address on the death certificate provided by the funeral home.

Having the very affordable Inman Travel Plan Coverage can help you avoid the hassles of unknown procedures. For a one-time life-time fee of $450 per person you receive coverage for the rest of your life. You and your loved ones and travel partners can have peace of mind and avoid crisis mode and major problems when you travel because you have the Travel Plan Coverage and paid for it ahead of time! Wake up, Travelers! Take control of your own life when it comes to necessary paperwork and procedures and planning ahead!

**Inman Travel (Protection) Plan Coverage website:**

https://inmantravelprotection.weebly.com/

**LINK to Application form:**

https://simplehpp.com/travelplan/?MFN=Helen&MLN=Scherrer-Diamond&MID=HESCM02&ME=helenscherrerdiamond@gmail.com

# Helen Scherrer-Diamond

AS THE COMMUNITY OUTREACH Director and "Networking Ninja" for two Atlanta funeral homes, Helen Scherrer-Diamond offers a diverse and highly skilled background. Born in Philadelphia, PA, Helen earned her degree in Business Administration and Communications at Muhlenberg College in Allentown, PA. Working at Honeywell during school vacations and an internship at IBM while in college, Helen was hired by IBM as an Administrative Assistant upon graduating, and worked directly with the sales department. With IT knowledge, sales skills, and the growing Internet, Helen was recruited by PA Blue Shield, later being promoted to Supervisor over 8 women in Group Insurance. Pursuing her career, Helen became self-employed with a marketing company, serving many small business owners in metro Atlanta during the Olympics. With changes in the Advertising industry, Helen accepted a position as Marketing Specialist with an agency of MassMutual. With management changes, Helen left and became an Estate Planning Rep with a local legal firm, helping families understand the importance of estate planning legal documents. Having lost her parents by age 28, Helen learned the importance of pre-planning for the inevitable. She obtained her Georgia Life and Health Insurance License and helps educate the community about planning ahead and important resources available.

Helen is a world traveler, having worked on an archaeological dig (Tel Akko) in Israel, and visiting Canada, Holland, Belgium, England, Ireland, and South Africa. Helen is currently a member of the Atlanta Chapter of NAIPC, and a member of Atlanta Senior Care Network Niche (ASCNN), and member of SRANA. Helen is married to David Diamond, a native of Atlanta, and has 3 adult stepsons.

# SOCIAL ISSUES

# Older Adults With Special Needs Children
## By Peter Klamkin

**Question:**

MY CHILD HAS special needs, and I'm concerned about what will happen when I pass away. What can I do to make sure he is taken care of after I'm gone?

**Answer:**

This book is special as it is primarily written by those who have first-hand knowledge and experience in their specific subject. The author of this chapter is no different.

The point of this book is two-fold. First, you need to know that you are not alone. You may think your situation is unique, however, with roughly 10,000 seniors turning 65 every day, the odds are there are others who have found themselves in what they thought was an untenable situation. Somehow, they learned and managed to persevere.

The second point is there will be times, no matter how much you think you understand the problems facing you, you'll need an expert. Much of what will be discussed here is based on three primary areas where you'll need a qualified expert to see your long term plans through.

Three come immediately to mind. First, and foremost, you are going to need an attorney. There are attorneys who specialize in helping parents navigate long term plans for special needs children, no matter their age.

The second is a qualified financial planner. Again, while you may be thinking about a short term situation, a good planner can get you prepared for the long haul.

Finally, you may need a good accountant, most certainly a CPA. An accountant and a financial planner can work in tandem to ensure your needs and those of your child (children) are met.

With these goals in mind, here are some of the difficult questions which are apt to arise. It would be impossible to address every situation. But these questions and answers are a useful and easy to use format to help guide you.

## Where Do I Begin?

You have to assess your situation. Often, with a special needs child, your goal is just to make it through the day. You are juggling so many things at once, making sure immediate needs are met.

For the purposes of this chapter, you have to think long-term. What could your situation look like a month from now, a year, five years, ten years, and so on. Most importantly, what will happen if I and/or my spouse is no longer able or here to be with my child? It's a difficult question, but one which needs to be addressed.

Age is the biggest factor. As your child turns 18, all legal rights go to your child. As with every situation in this section, know what your individual state requirements and laws are, and consult an attorney. There are those which specialize in guardianship law as well as those who specialize in working with medical disabilities and working with Social Security. Most importantly, find one who'll not only serve as your attorney, but your advocate.

## How Do I Find the Right Expert?

The easy answer is to search online but it's not that simple. The internet is a good place to start, but you likely know through support groups, friends with similar situations, your physicians, and networking, the right people to ask. Don't be afraid to ask, and most importantly, when you find an expert ask the questions you need answered. Come prepared with a detailed list as these people are likely to be with your child after you are gone. Prepare as if you are not going to be there.

Each state has agencies and programs to help you. Many programs go unnoticed, you have to ask. For instance, Texas has a program which reimburses private health insurance premiums to parents of special needs services. Your state may have it too, the best place to ask, again, is other parents in a similar situation to yours.

It should be noted no two situations are identical. Your child may have different needs. You may have another child who can care for their sibling once you are gone. Others may not be so fortunate. No matter what, dealing with this very important issue requires planning and difficult decision making, done best when you have your full faculties to make them. Be prepared.

## What Are the Important Needs for My Child?

Money: By now, if your child doesn't receive Social Security Income (SSI), get it. You may need an attorney, and you may be declined the first go round. Apply again, this time with some muscle behind you.

## Can your child partially support himself/herself? Will they be able to in the future?

The same goes for Medicaid. Make sure your child's medical needs are met long term. Chances are you have both SSI and Medicaid in place, but you need to be assured they will run long into the future. Programs and benefits are more apt to be cut these days, than added.

**Housing**: Where will my child live after I am gone? Will it be with family? Friends? A group home? Can my child live independently? Every situation is different as is every child. Nevertheless, it's as important as anything you will consider. Ask whether your child qualifies for Section 8 housing.

## Does It Make Sense to Have My Child Move Now?

Having your child living out of the house comfortably, safely, and having their needs met can offer you a tremendous amount of peace of mind. As you age it may be more difficult to manage your child's day to day needs. Knowing they are taken care of and presumably happy, will provide a tremendous amount of relief to you. It may be the most difficult thing you can do, letting your child go, but with it, knowing your child is protected.

## Who Do You Trust?

Protection of your plans and assets is key. Most importantly, your child should have a special needs trust. Again, an attorney who specializes in children with disabilities is the place to start. The trust can protect SSI and other funds. In most cases, funds left in a will eliminate SSI income. A trust is paramount. Any amount of money can go into it, but there are restrictions as to how the money is spent. Much like SSI.

You need to choose a trustee–someone has to manage your child's needs. This is another decision not to be taken lightly. If it is another child, make sure they know what the role of the trustee is. It should be someone with the expectation that they'll live longer than you. It can also be someone in a fiduciary role, again, your attorney is key.

## Who's My Best Advocate?

The answer is you. Nobody is as knowledgeable, resourceful, and especially passionate as you. Nobody knows your child as well as you.

But there will be times when you find yourself frustrated and in need. Use all and every resource available to you. Find the appropriate state agencies and take full advantage of the services and programs available to you.

If necessary, go to your local, state, and congressional representatives. Many have direct access to an ombudsman whose job it is to act on your behalf. Don't be afraid to make the call. They represent you.

Build a network. Are you part of a support group? If there isn't one, start one. To be certain, there are others who feel alone and need to know they are not.

## What Happens if I Do Nothing?

Your situation will not get better as you age. Plan ahead. Let this book be a starting point and guide. Seek help.

## Peter Klamkin

Peter is a 17 year veteran of the reverse mortgage business, with a combined career of 34 years of working in the senior marketplace. He has been an elected officer of two insurance companies and now serves as Vice-President, Business Leader/Reverse for Cardinal Financial, a major mortgage lender.

Peter began his career in the medical publishing business, first as a medical publishing sales representative and then as a medical editor for several medical publishers.

He is a member of the Board of Directors for the National Aging in Place Council (NAIPC) and is the host of the NAIPC podcast, "Hidden Gems in Aging." He has been an invited speaker for insurance and reverse mortgage industry meetings, a radio show guest, and a trusted resource in marketing in the senior space.

Peter has volunteered with the Make A Wish Foundation, the Muscular Dystrophy Association, the Easter Seals, and the United

Mitochondrial Disease Foundation, and is an Ambassador for the United Network of Organ Sharing (UNOS).

Peter has a focus on men as caregivers first through his father who was a caregiver for 26 years, and himself. He is the founder of "Ginger Ale Boy" a resource for men caregivers and "Referral Without Walls", a business networking group. He and his wife Susan reside in the Dallas area with their daughter, Emily, who currently is listed for a multi-visceral (five organ) transplant at the University of Miami.

He is a graduate of Franklin Pierce University, Rindge, New Hampshire.

# Cultural Considerations as Your Loved One Ages

By Jennifer Lagemann

**Question:**

HOW CAN I FIND an aging in place arrangement that suits my loved one's cultural needs? My wife is an Asian immigrant, and her native language is Vietnamese. With her dementia progressing, her English is regressing, and her Vietnamese is more apparent. Her cultural traditions and rituals span her diet, behavior, language, and more. I want to honor her life and wishes as she navigates her aging journey. How do I start the process?

**Answer:**

**Demographic Shifts in the US**

America has always been a melting pot of a country, and we are going to reach a point where minorities become the majority of the population. Families are also more dispersed and having less children, making older adults and solo-agers more dependent on auxiliary, professional support. Currently, the white-only population is 75% of America's makeup.[27]

Let's break this down a little bit more. With families being more dispersed, it will shift more adult children into long distance caregiving

---

27 (https://www.census.gov/quickfacts/fact/table/US/PST045222)

roles, and they'll play a large hand in the coordination of professional services.

With people having less children, the adult children will bear more responsibility than they historically have. Responsibilities generally fall on a primary caregiver, and they delegate to other siblings, but on the whole, the weight will be heavier moving forward. Many minority cultures embedded family caregiving into their culture, something that isn't native in the US, making it important for existing senior care resources to learn about the nuances and unique nature of each culture and how to best serve them. This also means that minority families with seniors will have a higher incidence of unpaid family caregiving, as opposed to native families who have a better experience with professional services.

The current and expected future need for auxiliary senior care services will prompt providers and partners to become culturally competent and learn how to best approach each family. The most concentrated age group of caregivers is seniors themselves, which creates an interesting opportunity for providers to help caregivers to feel supported enough that when they need care, they'll reach out to professional care services, too.

I fall into the minority culture group myself, with my mom and aunt who are both seniors from Asia. They live in Massachusetts, and I live out in the Midwest. I am currently navigating and finding resources that will be helpful to them in the future and wanted to share my knowledge and experience with you.

In 2021, immigrants made up 13% of the population, which will continue to increase, creating a need for more culturally diverse and culturally competent caregivers and senior care support systems.[28] Most

---

28 (https://www.migrationpolicy.org/article/frequently-requested-statistics-immigrants-and-immigration-united-states#:~:text=In%202021%2C%20immigrants%20comprised%2013.6,share%20they%20comprised%20in%202019.)

commonly, immigrants are coming from Mexico, El Salvador, Guatemala, India, Honduras, and China.[29] The care that older adults need from these and other countries requires a different skill set, training, and approach. Next, we'll talk about the importance of culturally competent senior care-related services.

## The Importance of Culturally Competent Services

The American healthcare and long-term care system was not created equally. The treatments, narratives, policies, and systems were created to interact with and engage the largest population group in the country: English-speaking people that subscribe to American culture.

This leaves a quarter of the current population to piecemeal and devise their own separate and disparate care support networks, comprised mostly of family support.

To engage the healthcare system, you must be able to read patient literature, understand what your doctor is saying, and, more importantly, providers must understand how you talk and behave and how that translates into tangible and intangible care needs. Moreover, even when patient literature is shared, it's often written above the average reading level, which may not be easily translated by a family member or caregiver.

For older adults from a different country who don't speak English natively or at all, they:

- Don't understand the patient literature without proper transcription or translation services
- Aren't communicated to properly by providers in a way that's easy to understand

---

29 (https://edition.cnn.com/2023/04/15/us/where-immigrants-come-from-cec/index.html#:~:text=Immigrants'%20top%20countries%20of%20origin%20in%20the%20United%20States&text=A%20Department%20of%20Homeland%20Security,%2C%20India%2C%20Honduras%20and%20China.)

- Aren't truly heard or seen by their providers to read between the lines and understand culturally specific responses or geographic nuances that might be unique to foreign-born patients.

Having culturally competent senior care services gives older adults what they deserve.

Let's also define what it means to have culturally competent care, according to the University of Pennsylvania, "The ability to relate effectively to individuals from various groups and backgrounds. Culturally competent services respond to the unique needs of members of minority populations and are also sensitive to the ways in which people with disabilities experience the world. Within the behavioral health system (which addresses both mental illnesses and substance abuse), cultural competence must be a guiding principle, so that services are culturally sensitive and provide culturally appropriate prevention, outreach, assessment, and intervention."[30]

What does this mean for older adults? They can eat the food that they like to eat; they can talk to their caregiver and ask questions in their native language; they can share common interests and cultural celebrations without it being awkward or uncomfortable.

There are also many consequences to care that is not culturally responsive:
- Care quality suffers
- Satisfaction scores are low
- Family members have to step in more than they should (it should be a choice)
- Communication often gets (literally) lost in translation.

Most languages don't translate squarely, especially regarding medical terminology. Dementia, in many cases, doesn't translate well.

---

30 (https://bhsd.sccgov.org/sites/g/files/exjcpb711/files/Cultural-Competency-with-Older-Adults.pdf)

For example, in many Asian and Native American languages, there is no word for dementia. This can create barriers to diagnosis leading to disproportionately negative care outcomes and undertreatment.

## How To Find Culturally Competent Senior Care Services

Finding senior care resources is difficult as it is and filtering out these services to find one(s) that support your cultural needs is harder. Luckily for you, I've been in your shoes and have prepared a few tips to help you get started.

**Join neighborhood groups:** Word of mouth is a powerful way to start any decision-making process. Facebook is a great place to start finding your tribe and community to find care and support from people like you who have been in your shoes before. You'll likely find a few people who speak your language or can help you with what you need. I see many residents in towns offering their truck to plow out snow in driveways, moms offering to cook extra meals for folks in need, and more. Your community can show up for you if you seek them in the right places. There might be places online and offline that you can utilize, like a community center or non-profit that is geared toward aging resources.

**Find your culture in non-culture-specific resources:** Google is one search engine of man. You can search for resources on Reddit, online support groups, and more. Meal delivery services, for example, now offer culturally diverse options with gluten-free and heart-friendly menus. They might not advertise their services online as "Mandarin cuisine options" but if you look at their menus, you will likely find a few dishes that you like. Some home care agencies I know of put the languages their caregivers speak on their website, so even if a resource doesn't specify that they serve your culture, they might be able to help you. There are, however, many resources that do specify that they support various cultures. For example, Apna Ghar is a home care agency in Michigan that specializes in caring for Indian people, while Vietwell Home Care offers Vietnamese home health services in Texas.

**Search for specialized senior living providers that care for your community.** This is a little bit tricky, but it can be done! Many people are bilingual, and with the nature of Duolingo and other language learning programs, staff members can be trained to speak the words and phrases you may need. I worked in a senior living community with a brother and sister that only spoke Portuguese, and we communicated through non-verbal gestures, printouts, and the use of a whiteboard to draw pictures, etc.

**Seek out educational resources for senior care offered in your native language.** If you find someone that speaks your language but maybe they don't have formal caregiver training, they can engage in a virtual training session that helps them understand the basics. Some of these platforms include Care Academy and Nevvon.

There are no perfect ways to assemble your care support team, but culturally competent care is within reach. Use these tips as a starting point to your journey, and you will open the door to care options that think, act, and behave like you do.

## Jennifer Lagemann

Caregiving and Senior Care Writer/Marketer
Founder, NextJenn Copy

JENNIFER LAGEMANN IS A former family caregiver, and home care agency administrator. She currently serves as a fractional CMO to companies in the senior care space, living in Kansas with her husband, Destry. Jenn's worked with companies like TCARE, Care Academy, and home care businesses of all sizes, mostly in the franchise space. Her passion for this space came from caring for her grandmother when she lived in Massachusetts, as she learned how difficult the long-term care system was to navigate. This turned Jenn's familial hardship into a career, helping families across the country and internationally to find the care that they need and deserve. She currently writes for Forbes Health, the American Society on Aging, and McKnight's Home Care, and previously wrote for the Kansas City Star.

Portfolio: https://muckrack.com/jennifer-lagemann-1
Website: https://nextjenncopy.com/

## Difficult Aging in Place Conversations

# Deciding Who Will Take Care of Your Elderly Family Member

By Wayne Mitchell

**Question:**

WHEN IT COMES TO caring for an elderly family member, it can be a difficult decision to determine whether to bring in a caregiver or to take on the responsibility as a family. What are the factors to consider when making this decision, and how do I carefully weigh each one to ensure that the best decision is made for the elderly person's well-being?

**Answer:**

Many times, we are not prepared for the tasks of caring for and providing personal care for an elderly family member. It can be a difficult time for both the adult child and the elderly family member. The situation can become very complex and emotional depending on the individual situation and the relationships with their elderly family members and siblings.

It's normal for the adult child to experience various emotions, keeping in mind the elderly family member may also be having similar emotions. There are many emotions we may experience throughout the process of caring for an elderly family member such as responsibility, anxiety, sadness, loss, guilt, appreciation, love, empathy, and a feeling of being overwhelmed. It is my hope that the following will help you overcome many of these emotions and understand that it is okay to ask for and accept assistance during this difficult time.

I have broken the question into three different scenarios that may overlap, but all fall into common expression of "Aging in Place" wherever it may be.

- When the elderly family member lives close to family and wants to remain in their home.
- When an elderly family member lives a distance from family and wants to remain in their home.
- When an elderly family member decides that they do not want to remain home and consider moving to a senior community.

**Here are some factors to consider when the elderly person lives close by family and wants to remain in their home:**

- **Level of care needed:** Assess the level of care your elderly family members require. This can be determined by having a healthcare professional who has geriatric experience such as a primary care physician, healthcare specialist, registered nurse, a certified geriatric care provider, or even a company that specializes in providing in-home senior care. Many of these professionals understand the differences between what your elderly family members are requesting versus what they need. Many family members want to provide the care needed. However, if elderly family members require constant care, then it may not be feasible for family members to provide this care on their own. In such cases, bringing in a professional caregiver can be the best decision.
- **Family member availability:** Consider the availability of family members to provide care. Determine whether you or other family members can take on the caregiving responsibilities, either by living with your elderly family members or through frequent

visits. This option may require careful coordination and planning among family members. If all family members have busy work schedules or live far away, it may be challenging to understand and provide the necessary care.

- **Caregiver qualifications:** If you decide to hire a caregiver, it's important to ensure that the caregiver you hire has the qualifications and training to provide the necessary level of care required by your elderly family members. This may include certifications in caregiving, nursing, specialized training for specific conditions, and being properly trained to handle any medical needs and emergencies. In addition, check with your attorney and tax professionals to review the general liability and tax consequences you or your elderly family members may be exposed to.

- **Cost:** Hiring a professional caregiver can be expensive, so it's important to factor in the cost of hiring a caregiver when making your decision. Consider your budget and the cost of various caregiving options before making a decision. Investigate what types of insurance are available such as long-term care insurance or government programs that support home care. Keep in mind that hiring a professional caregiver agency may be more costly than hiring an independent caregiver. However, the professional caregiving agency has the staff available, ensures that the caregivers are qualified and have the proper liability insurance. Ask the professional caregiver agency and the independent caregiver to show proof of any state licensing, worker compensation insurance (if state mandated), general liability insurance along with current references, and criminal background checks.

- **Electronic alert system:** Install a quality electronic medical alert system that requires minimal maintenance and utilizes monitoring and GPS capabilities. Many of these systems have a pendant that is worn around the neck or a wrist band that can either detect a fall and will automatically call for help, or a simple push of a button will call for help. Many alert systems may not charge for hardware and charge a monthly fee.

- **Elderly person's preferences:** Finally, it's important to consider the elderly person's preferences. Some people may prefer to receive care from family members, while others may be more comfortable with a professional caregiver.

**When the elderly family members live a distance away, are showing signs of needing assistance, and want to remain in their home, there are several options to consider:**

- **Hire a caregiver:** You can consider hiring a professional caregiver to help your elderly family members with their daily needs. This can include assistance with ADLs such as bathing, dressing, grooming, and meal preparation. A caregiver can either live-in or come in for a few hours a day, depending on your elderly family members' needs. When selecting a caregiver, ensure they are qualified as covered in the previous section under Caregiver Qualifications. If you consider a Caregiver Agency, check to see if they offer the ability for you to review the plan of care and caregiver notes online through a family portal. This allows you to be kept informed of your elderly family member's needs and care.

- **Home modification:** Have a safety assessment done on your elderly family members' home. This can be done by a local community senior service agency, home health, visiting nurse team, geriatric manager, or a senior home care agency. Utilizing this safety assessment, you can consider modifying your elderly

family members' home to make it more accessible and safer. This can include installing grab bars, wheelchair ramps, and other modifications that can help your elderly family members navigate their home more easily.
- **Telehealth services:** Explore telehealth services that allow your elderly family members to connect with healthcare professionals remotely. This can include virtual doctor visits, remote monitoring of vital signs, and medication management. Telehealth can provide convenient access to healthcare and reduce the need for frequent in-person visits.
- **Community resources:** Many communities offer resources for elderly individuals, such as transportation services, meal delivery, and senior centers. These resources can help your elderly family members maintain their independence while also receiving the support they need.

**If the elderly family members decide they do not want to remain in their home and choose the option of moving into an assisted living community:**
- **Assisted living facilities:** Assisted living facilities are residential facilities that provide care and support services to elderly individuals. They offer various levels of care, including assistance with ADLs, medication management, and medical services. Many also offer an independent living service (ILS) when your elderly family member lives in an apartment-like setting where they can go to the dining hall for meals and enjoy various activities all while having the assurance that, if they need assistance in an emergency, help would be nearby. It's important to consider the specific needs and preferences of your elderly family members when deciding which option is best for them. You can also

consult with healthcare professionals or eldercare specialists for guidance on the best option to choose.

Ultimately, the best decision will depend on the individual circumstances of the family and the elderly family member. It is best to consult with a healthcare professional, eldercare specialist, or a senior care agency to help you make an informed decision.

## Wayne Mitchell

MY STORY IS LIKE many that are in the senior care field. As my parents aged it became clearer they needed some assistance that I wasn't able to provide at that time due to living in another state. As I tried to find experienced caring assistance for them, I found my search very difficult and confusing. It was then that I decided there has to be a better way. I wanted to provide the best care I could, just as my parents provided for me, my entire life.

As an award-winning leader with extensive business administration, business team development, and exceptional customer service skills, I decided to open Caring Senior Service of Northern Virginia to provide not only the best senior care but also become a resource for seniors, their spouses, and their families as they navigate through the aging process.

I am so proud of this great team of caring, kindhearted individuals that are helping make my dream a reality. They are using a proven process called the GreatCare Method which was developed by Caring

Senior Service while caring for seniors for over 30 years. By combining our GreatCare Method with First in Class technology and introducing AI, we keep seniors connected with family, their care team and healthcare professionals. Together we are able to make a true difference in the lives of the seniors as they choose to age in place, wherever that may be, and their families we serve.

**Wayne Mitchell**
Owner, Caring Senior Service of Northern Virginia

**LinkedIn:**
https://www.linkedin.com/in/wmitchell/

**Facebook:**
CSSNorthernVirginia
N/A

**Business website:**
www.NovaSeniorCare.com
N/A

**YouTube channel:**
https://www.youtube.com/c/CaringSeniorServiceHQ
N/A

**Other resources to share:**
*https://tinyurl.com/LikeFamily*
*https://issuu.com/cssnova/docs/why_we_care_booklet/s/13224088*

# Protecting Privacy

By Heather Nickerson

**Question:**

My wife and I have heard a lot about needing to protect our privacy as we get older, but it's not an easy conversation to have together. She is very trusting in others and wants to help anyone and everyone that she can! I am not as trusting of others, and to me, protecting our privacy seems like a daunting task. Any advice for how to start, and what to do to help avoid being victims of identity theft as we age?

**Answer:**

Privacy is a basic human right. We all love it. We all want it, and yet, we don't always know how to go about protecting it, especially as we get older. Technologies change, new threats emerge, and it gets harder and harder to safeguard our personal information with all the digital sharing and oversharing that is ever-present in our society.

Want to save on your next grocery bill? Sign up for Amazon Prime and link your Prime Account to your Whole Foods account. Seeing the doctor tomorrow? Fill out these five forms in triplicate and don't forget to include your Social Security Number. Want to help your grandchild secure their first apartment? Submit two years of tax returns via email, and a copy of your most recent bank statement to prove you have sufficient funds to serve as a guarantor.

These are all real-life situations we may encounter daily, monthly, or once in a blue moon. Chances are we wouldn't think twice about any of the above requests. They all seem legitimate, and they all seem to be harmless in the grand scheme of things.

That said, these mundane requests could open us up to the unintended and unwanted consequences of identity theft. Whole Foods or Amazon could be the victim of a cyber breach or hack, and with it, goes your personal information. There could be an unscrupulous or disgruntled employee at your doctor's office who uses your personal information (and your Social Security Number) for their own gain. And although well intentioned, sending personal and financial information via a non-secure email account puts you at risk—you have no way of knowing where that email (and those attachments) will go in the future, and who will eventually gain access to your information.

Keep in mind that the goal for any identity thief is to collect your Social Security Number and other personal identifying information, such as your full legal name, date of birth, and current address. When combined, these details provide a thief with all they need to steal your identity.

The Federal Trade Commission reports that 20 percent of the victims that report identity theft are over 60[31]. Why target those age 60+? Chances are if you are over 60, you have built up a good credit score over your lifetime, and you have some savings on hand, both in regular checking and savings accounts, as well as retirement accounts.

You may also be more trusting. In a study by the Massachusetts Institute of Technology[32], people were asked, "Do you feel that most people can be trusted?" So-called boomers, born 1946 to 1964, gave the

---

31 https://www.ftc.gov/system/files/ftc_gov/pdf/P144400OlderConsumersReportFY22.pdf
32 https://www.forbes.com/sites/nextavenue/2016/12/18/why-older-adults-are-so-susceptible-to-financial-fraud/?sh=1efdc9f72770

highest percentage of "Yes" answers. The bad guys know this and try to exploit these traits.

So, what can you do to protect your privacy, and ensure matrimonial harmony and a happy medium for both you and your spouse? Yes, there is a way to trust in and support others, and still keep your privacy top of mind. We'll address some simple tips to protect your privacy in the next section, and then close out the chapter with a section of possible conversation starters.

## Tips to Protect Your Privacy

**Think twice before giving out your Social Security Number.** Do you know you are not required to enter your Social Security Number on medical forms? Sure, doing so makes it easier for office staff to quickly locate your medical records, but you could just as easily ask them to use your insurance number, first and last name, and date of birth, etc. Really, anything but your Social Security Number. Same goes for most other forms that may request your Social Security Number. Your Social Security Number is only ever required for employment forms, to receive Social Security, and some additional government services. That's it.

**Never email financial or personal identifying information (PII).** So much of our daily lives are conducted over email or online, it's easy to lose sight of the information that we send and resend as each new request comes in. That said, not all emails are secure. Bad guys can intercept or otherwise gain access to your email and the information contained therein. If you are conducting financial, legal, medical, or other important correspondence and transactions online, think twice before responding with your personal identifying information, especially your Social Security Number. The best option is uploading that information to a secure website or portal where it is viewable (and trackable) by both parties. If the party you are dealing with asks you to email them your information, ask them first if they have a secure portal where you can upload the information. Chances are they probably do if you are dealing with a large bank, brokerage, or medical office. If they don't? Suggest a phone call or other secure means of transmitting the information.

**Establish a family code word.** The bad guys have quickly learned how to use Artificial Intelligence (AI) to scam others. One of the more recent scams involves using your voice (or fragments of your voice) to create a realistic "ask for help" from a loved one. A common example is a grandparent receiving a call from a grandchild, saying they are traveling overseas and need help getting back home. Could you please wire them money for a plane ticket. Sounds compelling, but chances are your grandchild is safe and sound at home or in their college dorm, not stranded halfway around the world. The best way to avoid being a victim of these scams? Establish a family code word that can be used to verify that the person on the other end of the phone really is your beloved grandchild. Code words can be simple words or phrases such as "golden retriever" or "orange tabby cat." Avoid using words or phrases that are personally identifiable or could be guessed after a quick Google search of you or your family.

**Create strong passwords and use a password manager.** Most cyber security experts recommend you create a password that is between 18 and 26 characters in length, and contains at least one upper case letter, one lower case letter, one number, and one special character. That may sound overwhelming right now, but it is much easier than it sounds. Think of a short sentence or an easy to remember phrase, such as "my grandkid is the best." Following the above advice, that simple phrase can easily be turned into the password, "MyGr@ndK1d1sTh3B3st!" Easy to remember, much harder for a hacker to compromise.

And for those of you that don't want to worry about having to remember if it is a "!" or a "1", password managers can help. What is a password manager you might ask? Think of it as a digital safe for all of your passwords. A password manager will generate, retrieve, and keep track of your passwords across countless accounts for you, while also protecting all your vital online info—not only passwords but PINs, credit-card numbers, and their three-digit CVV codes, answers to security questions, and more—with encryption so strong that it might take a hacker decades, if not centuries, to crack.

**Use two-factor authentication on all financial and medical accounts.** This is one of the simplest ways to protect your privacy. Two-factor authentication requires that you validate that it's really you that's trying to login to your account and not some bad guy by providing a second way (i.e., "factor") for that validation. Choose the option that works best for you—whether that is a text message, phone call, or email verification. Some two-factor authentication sites also allow you to scan a QR code to validate that it is really you. Take an hour to set this up on all your accounts, today.

**Limit access to your credit cards and other personal information.** Do you have help around your house? Cleaning crews? Visiting nurses? In-home physical therapy sessions? Don't leave your credit cards or other personal information (bank statements, credit card statements, tax returns, etc.) laying out and about where others can easily see them. It is unfortunate but true, identity theft can happen in your home by the ones you may trust the most. Eliminate the risk of this happening to you by keeping your personal, financial, medical, and other details safely out of sight.

**When in doubt, shred, don't toss.** Inundated with unwanted credit card, reverse mortgage, and loan offers? Your first reaction may be toss them in the trash but shredding them is a better decision as some of those offers require only a signature to activate. You don't want those offers falling into the wrong hands. The same goes for copies of medical records, bank statements, credit card statements, and the like. Anything that you have laying around that contains your personal identifying information or your financial account information. Shredding will prevent a bad guy from co-opting your information and stealing your identity.

## Conversation Starters

The great (and easy) part about this is that you don't have to be the bad guy here and bring up an unwanted topic. Turn on the news or open the latest AARP Bulletin, and chances are you are going to come face to face with an elder fraud story. Use this (and all the ongoing press around identity theft) to your advantage. Start with a headline-gripping issue and make it personal.

Hey dear, did you hear what they said on the news last night about the latest advances in AI and how scammers are now using AI to claim they are holding your loved one hostage? I wouldn't want that to happen to us, what do you think we should do?

Or

Did you read the latest article in the AARP Bulletin? I was shocked to learn that identity thieves are filing fraudulent tax returns using senior citizens Social Security Numbers. I've been thinking about how often we give out our Social Security Number, maybe we should talk about that?

You could also start with the facts as noted earlier in this chapter, or, if your spouse is the ultra-altruistic type, appeal to that side of them.

Sally, I know you want to help all the grandkids with their first apartment. We'll need to make sure our credit scores stay strong and that our identities are not compromised if we are going to be guarantors for years to come. What do you say we start doing a quarterly privacy check-up to make sure our information is as safe as it can be so we can keep helping our family?

## Protecting Privacy

At the end of the day, it's your information (and your privacy). Protect it! Think twice before emailing or sharing your personal identifying information, social security number included, and establish a family code word to avoid falling victim to common-place scams. On the tech side, set up two-factor authentication for all digital financial and medical accounts, and double check that you are using a different strong password to access those accounts. Be careful about what documents you have out around the house, viewable to all, and when in doubt, shred sensitive information rather than tossing it in the trash. These simple steps will help you lead a more secure, private life as you age in place.

# Heather Nickerson

**HEATHER NICKERSON** IS the co-founder and CEO of **Artifcts**. She is an avid hiker, skier, baker, storyteller, and collector of memories. Prior to co-founding Artifcts, Heather served as President of a private security company and authored a book on how to protect your privacy. She also served for nearly a decade as an intelligence analyst with the Central Intelligence Agency (CIA), including serving as a briefer in a war zone tour in Afghanistan.

**Business website**

Artifcts.com

**LinkedIn**

https://www.linkedin.com/in/heather-nickerson/

# Getting Help for Difficult People
## By Jennifer Prell

**Question:**

WE COME INTO THE world kicking and screaming and leave this world kicking and screaming. "I'm leaving my home feet first! My kids can take care of everything after I'm dead." Planning now for future needs is extremely important. Aging with pain, illness, and cognitive decline can limit one's ability to communicate effectively, with purpose, and receive the necessary help to move forward. How do I handle it if my elderly parents become difficult to deal with?

**Answer:**

My team assisted a client whose widowed father was living independently at home with the assistance of a cleaning lady who visited every two weeks. He had never discussed what he wanted as he aged other than talking about his retirement fund.

On the surface, those who saw him regularly thought he was doing fine. As time went on, he developed macular degeneration, his body grew tired, he slowed down, stopped exercising, and socializing. He did eat well as his daughter made him meals he could reheat. He was able to drive to the grocery store and make other purchases as needed.

Things moved along quietly until his son really took a thorough look around the house. What he discovered was alarming. There was a large amount of dust on the floorboards, the master bathroom was filthy with feces around the toilet, dust on top of the shower, mold on the windowsills, and in the refrigerator. He was appalled at the poor performance of the cleaning lady! She was taking advantage of his dad, and he felt angry and disgusted. It was obvious that his dad wasn't doing that great at home, and he wasn't thriving.

Knowing that action was needed, the son spoke with his sister about the possibility of his dad moving into some type of senior housing. They reached out to me for guidance. After gathering all the necessary information to determine the best level of care, location, amenities sought, and the budget, I deduced that their father could move into an independent living situation that would provide a safer environment, meals, and socialization. I referred them to a few communities that met his profile and set up the tours. After personal visits and research, they narrowed the options down to two communities and they brought their dad to each building to tour. The adult children discussed the options with their father. He reviewed the two communities the children presented. He toured them and decided on one that had many men living in it, as it had opportunities to play cards and had great meals. He was willing to give the new lifestyle a try.

He absolutely thrived! He attended activities, played cards with some new friends, ate healthy meals, and gained a lot of energy from the positive benefits of socialization and exercise. In fact, his children couldn't talk with him during the day, because he was too busy! This was a very good outcome, but sometimes conversations don't always go this well.

Humans don't listen to one another for a variety of reasons. Some are quick to reject advice, refuse to plan for impending needs, or even become combative when approached about the future. We only want the best for them, so why aren't they listening?

# Getting Help for Difficult People

If your loved one is obstinate, they may need a longer on-ramp to conclude they need help. Creatures of habit don't like change or being told what to do. If this is the situation, it's best to ease into the conversation about getting help and the living options. Sometimes making it their idea vs. your own helps move them forward. Primarily the goals are to engage in-home caregivers or help transition an older adult to a safer and more fulfilling senior community. A conversation can go something like this: "Dad, did you know that Joe Smith moved into a new senior community? He told me he loves the food, plays cards with the guys, and life is good! Do you want to go see him and maybe check out how he's living?" Talking about situations, raising ideas, or even suggesting having dinner at a senior community might help your loved one think about the future. Achieving a successful transition must come from the individual.

Difficult as it is to witness, some people may not understand the severity of their situation and think everything is fine the way it is. They don't see the house falling apart around them or that their memory loss and falls are not normal. Persons living with dementia don't have the capability to understand that their safety is at risk and can't make clear decisions. Others are frozen in fear of losing their independence, their ability to do whatever they want, or even selling the home is viewed as catastrophic. They can't objectively perceive the necessity of change, so acting out and pushing back are the tactics to avoid the inevitable.

How then, can we help people do what is necessary, so they are safe and able to thrive? Use your knowledge of the person and the support resources in your area to help them make educated and healthy decisions. Listen to what your loved one is saying to you. Are they putting up walls because they are afraid, don't know how to make the decision, or are simply satisfied living the way they are living? Make sure you respond to whatever's being said in an open and friendly manner. Don't judge, engage in arguments, or condescend, rather lift their spirits with opportunities, new friendships, activities, and safe, reliable care or housing.

Offer local resource professionals who offer objective counsel regarding home adaptability, caregiving agencies, handymen, transportation, and other senior-friendly services. If they want to transition to a new senior living opportunity refer them to a not-for-profit agency for information, referrals, and guidance for the best senior housing based on their needs. The focus should be on the person(s) moving. The discussion should include their current health and physical status, location requirements, amenities sought, budget, and other pertinent information. Suggesting advice from elder law attorneys to review their current documents, or create new ones; work with Senior Real Estate Specialist (SRES) Realtors to provide information for selling their home; enlist a (SMM) Senior Move Manager to help with sorting, packing, and moving, as well as cleaning out the home; and partnering with other senior specialty organizations that can assist in transitioning out of their current home and into a new one.

If nothing is helping the person decide from a safety and security standpoint, there are steps you can take to help them. If the person is over the age of 65, are neglecting themselves, or have diminished capacity, the Power of Attorney (POA) for Property and Healthcare (their representative) needs to find a solution that addresses their care needs, be it at home or in a new senior living environment. If there is no POA in place, then emergency Guardianship should be obtained through an elder law attorney. The attorney will file a motion and a judge will set a priority hearing for those who are at-risk. This is a costly and stressful solution, but necessary. Once the judge hears the case, he will assign a Guardian which will either be a family member, friend, or a Guardian ad Litem (assigned attorney).

If there is no family or friends that can help the senior, or if there are family dynamics in play, a report to Adult Protective Services (APS) or a police social worker will have to be made. APS and the police social worker will check in on the senior to investigate the claim. If they find that the senior is not safe at home, they will remove them to a safe place.

Aging conversations should start at an early age, so everyone knows what their loved ones want as they get older. This should include what city and state they prefer to live in, the activities they'd like to continue doing, their budget, and their Advance Directives should they get sick and not be able to make a decision for themselves.

Being a loving, adult child includes being more supportive and direct as needed.

Elderwerks Educational Services is a not-for-profit 501(c)3 organization offering complimentary senior living coordination, advocacy, and education; we are "senior guidance advisors." The advisors work directly with you to help figure out the best options for your needs. Have an aging question? Call Elderwerks first at 855-462-0100 or visit Elderwerks.org for more information.

## Jennifer Prell

JENNIFER PRELL
    President & Founder Elderwerks Educational Services
    Jennifer.prell@elderwerks.org
    https://www.elderwerks.org

    http://linkedin.com/company/elderwerks
    https://www.facebook.com/elderwerks
    https://www.instagram.com/elderwerks/
    https://www.youtube.com/c/ElderwerksEducationalServices

    https://www.elderwerks.org/directory/index.html

# Being Prepared
## By Kelly Rogers

**Question:**

Even when we think we are prepared for things, once an incident occurs, we find that we're more than likely not as prepared as we had thought. As a proactive person who is always well-prepared, what things do I need to do to keep from being overwhelmed?

**Answer:**

Whether you're a proactive person or a procrastinator, it seems to be more overwhelming than anticipated when things happen that we didn't account for. Even if we're well-prepared, what can I say? We are all human, and life and its crazy course is a fluid motion that is unique to each person. It's kind of hard to be 100% fully prepared with so many variables, huh?

As a previous Resource Specialist and active Gerontologist, I felt it was my duty, honor, and responsibility to be highly educated and helpful in both proactive/preventative and reactive/responsive situations equally. It didn't take long to learn that even a skilled and educated resource specialist in her own hometown still couldn't prevent pure chaos in times of need, even when the family was "prepared."

This brings me to my most recent true story:

(We will refer to this couple as Mr. & Mrs. Jones)

## Difficult Aging in Place Conversations

Mr. Jones has been caring for his elderly wife in their family home of many years in Indianapolis. Mrs. Jones is very active, however suffers from dementia and Alzheimer's and requires constant reminders, care, and supervision. Their son lives far away in Colorado and is an educated Financial Planner who specializes in helping seniors plan for the cost of retirement and aging in place. He even brought in a local Certified Gerontologist to help prepare and discuss the best steps, resources, and actions to take to keep both Mr. & Mrs. Jones aging in their home safely. Many times, we find that the adult children no longer live near mom and dad, and we have senior spouses caring for one another. This frequently leads to the older caregiving spouse then becoming the one who needs care.

The Gerontologist was amazing and went over many things to prepare them for a safer aging in place plan, including an assessment of the house to ensure it was safe and modified accordingly, respite care, local resources and services to bring in, all of their various housing and care options to choose from in their local community, and even reviewed the importance of setting up monitoring equipment in the home. Since no other family lived in Indianapolis anymore, this was a way for other loved ones to check in on them as well. All these experts came into the home to create a personalized assessment, care/resource plan and "prepare" Mr. & Mrs. Jones for aging success. But we all know how the saying goes… *you can lead a horse to water, but you can't make them to drink.*

Although they were professionally guided, prepared and had been savvy with their retirement funds and could easily afford any of the options presented, Mr. Jones did not want an *invasion of privacy* in his home (my dad would be the same way). Therefore, he chose not to utilize any of the recommendations, and they went back to their normal routine. Their son returned back home to Colorado and felt upset about his dad not taking any immediate action. Still, he felt better than when he arrived

# Being Prepared

now that he was impowered from meeting with the Gerontologist and the buffet of resources and options at their fingertips.

Five days later, the son received a call. "We don't know how to tell you this, but your father has passed away and your mother, due to her dementia, has been sitting at his bedside at home, holding his hand in confusion as he laid deceased in bed for five days."

I would like to say that nobody was prepared for this. Although the Gerontologist had actually brought up the topic when speaking to Mr. Jones and his son about how oftentimes we see the "healthier" senior caregiving spouse become the one who needs care or even passes sooner than expected, they still weren't prepared. This almost exact scenario was played out by the Gerontologist and discussed in full only one week prior to Mr. Jones passing with various solutions presented like respite care, virtual monitoring devices, in-home care services, etc. Little did anyone know (even though recently prepared and discussed) that this would play out as it did.

Being truly 100% prepared is almost impossible, but we can educate ourselves on relevant resources that match our situation and ways to motivate even the most stubborn, private, or difficult persons. We do this by balancing patience and respect with something I call Emotional Core Value Questions to implement critical thinking. Sometimes telling someone how things can play out doesn't have as much impact as asking them questions that lead them to their own answers on what's best. This includes the hard decision of having to invade someone's privacy if it means keeping a loved one safer. It must be their conclusion that they draw. When they come to their own self-realization, that motivates them to take action by having self-ownership in the decision. We can lead them better by asking the right questions more so than just giving and presenting them with the answer. In other words, be prepared.

## Kelly Rogers

Kelly Rogers is a Certified Gerontologist with more than 28 years of experience working with seniors and their families. She has a strong passion to educate and advocate for seniors, and her background in both senior care and financing makes her a perfect fit as the Head of Aging in Place Partnerships at Longbridge Financial, LLC. As a previous Senior Care Agency owner and co-founder, she uniquely understands the many challenges that agencies and seniors face. This experience has ignited a spark in her to educate people about additional ways to overcome the retirement and senior care crisis. Kelly is passionate about assisting seniors, their families, and care providers through the inclusion of housing wealth in retirement and care planning. This approach allows a higher quality of life, greater caregiver retention, better care for our seniors, and prevents costly and unnecessary hospital re-admittances. Kelly's drive in life is truly helping seniors and their families understand how they can afford the proper services and care they deserve.

krogers@longbridge-financial.com

# RESOURCES

## Aging Acronyms and Glossary

Activities of Daily Living (ADLs) – daily self-care activities, such as bathing, showering, and grooming

Advanced Directives – legal documents that provide instruction for medical care should you be unable to communicate your wishes (e.g., living will, durable power of attorney for health care)

Advocate, Healthcare – a professional who works with older adults and families to ensure health care plans and wishes are addressed

Accessory Dwelling Unit (ADU) – an additional housing unit on a single-family residential lot

Annual Enrollment Period (AEP) – a period of time during which the insured may make changes to their health insurance plans

Aging in Place (AIP) – the ability to live in a home of one's choosing in a safe and comfortable manner, regardless of age, income, geographic location, or ability level, as independently as possible

Aging in Place Planning – establishing a plan that allows you to maintain as much control as possible over future medical and lifestyle choices by researching your options now, and continually reviewing and modifying your plan as medical, financial, or other situations change

Assisted Living (AL) – communities that provide some type of assistance on a daily basis, such as housekeeping, nursing, and/or meals

Board Certified – indicates a doctor is qualified for specialization by one of the certification boards

Caregiver / Care Partner – a paid or unpaid support workers that assists with activities of daily living

Caregiver Support Group – a group that meets regularly to discuss a diagnosis with which your loved one has been diagnosed or to discuss caregiving in general

Case Manager – case managers are healthcare professionals who serve as patient advocates to support, guide and coordinate care for patients, families, and caregivers as they navigate their health and wellness journeys (source: https://cmsa.org/who-we-are/what-is-a-case-manager/)

Continuing Care Retirement Community (CCRC) – a community that offers multiple levels of care on one location, typically independent living, assisted living, memory care, and skilled nursing and rehabilitation

Conservator / Conservatorship – a situation when a judge must appoint another person to act or make decisions for another individual. The person the judge appoints is called the conservator. (source: https://selfhelp.courts.ca.gov/conservatorships)

Diagnosis, Terminal – a disease that cannot be cured and will cause death

Durable Medical Equipment (DME) – equipment and supplies ordered by a health care provider for everyday or extended use, e.g. oxygen equipment, wheelchairs, crutches, or blood testing strips for diabetics

Do Not Resuscitate (DNR) – indicates to your doctors and other healthcare providers that you don't want CPR attempted in the event your heart stops beating or your breathing stops (source: https://my.clevelandclinic.org/health/articles/8866-do-not-resuscitate-orders)

End-of-Life Wishes – your priorities and hopes for your care near the end-of-life

Executor – a person named in a will as taking legal responsibility for fulfilling the instructions left by the deceased regarding their estate. If there's no will, or those named are unwilling or unable to fulfil the executor role, a court may appoint an administrator in their place. (source: https://www.legalandgeneral.com/insurance/over-50-life-insurance/wills)

Fiduciary – someone who manages money or property for another

# RESOURCES

Geriatric Care Manager – professionals, sometimes called aging life care managers, are usually licensed nurses or social workers trained in caring for older adults. They act as private advocates and guides for family members who want to ensure their loved one is in the best hands, and they generally serve clients and families whose incomes are too high to qualify for publicly financed services. (source: https://www.aarp.org/caregiving/basics/info-2020/geriatric-care-manager.html)

Health Insurance Portability and Accountability Act of 1996 (HIPAA) – a federal law that required the creation of national standards to protect sensitive patient health information from being disclosed without the patient's consent or knowledge (source: https://www.cdc.gov/phlp/publications/topic/hipaa.html)

Hospice – focuses on the care, comfort, and quality of life of a person with a serious illness who is approaching the end-of-life (source: https://www.nia.nih.gov/health/what-are-palliative-care-and-hospice-care#hospice)

Health Savings Account (HSA) – a type of savings account that lets you set aside money on a pre-tax basis to pay for qualified medical expenses

Independent Living (IL) – communities that provide access to dining, medical care, entertainment, and other amenities

Licensed Practical Nurse (LPN) – a healthcare professional who performs basic medical tasks, such as checking vital signs and feeding patients

Long Term Care Hospitals (LTCH) – hospitals that focus on patients who, on average, stay more than 25 days. Many of the patients in LTCHs are transferred there from an intensive or critical care unit. (source: https://www.medicare.gov/Pubs/pdf/11347-Long-Term-Care-Hospitals.pdf)

Long Term Care Insurance (LTCI) – insurance designed to cover long-term services and supports, including personal and custodial care in a variety of settings such as a home, a community organization, or other facility. Policies reimburse policyholders a daily amount (up to a pre-selected limit) for services to assist them with activities of daily living such as bathing, dressing, or eating. (source: https://acl.gov/ltc/costs-and-who-pays/what-is-long-term-care-insurance)

Medicare Advantage (MA) – a health plan option, sometimes called Medicare Part C or MA Plans, approved by Medicare, and offered by private insurance companies

Memory Care (MC) – a community that offers specialized care for those living with Alzheimer's or another form of progressive-degenerative dementia

Mild Cognitive Impairment (MCI) – an early stage of memory loss or other cognitive ability loss (such as language or visual/spatial perception) in individuals who maintain the ability to independently perform most activities of daily living (source: https://www.alz.org/alzheimers-dementia/what-is-dementia/related_conditions/mild-cognitive-impairment)

Mobility – the ability of a patient to change and control their body position. Physical mobility requires sufficient muscle strength and energy, along with adequate skeletal stability, joint function, and neuromuscular synchronization. (source: https://www.ncbi.nlm.nih.gov/)

Medical Orders for Life-Sustaining Treatment (MOLST) – a set of medical orders for patients with advanced illness who might die within 1-2 years, require long-term care services, or wish to avoid and/or receive specific life-sustaining treatments now (source: https://molst.org)

Nursing Care Plans (NCP) – a plan that contains relevant information about a patient's diagnosis, the goals of treatment, the specific nursing orders (including what observations are needed and what actions must be performed), and an evaluation plan (source: https://nurse.org/articles/what-are-nursing-care-plans/)

Occupational Therapy (OT) – uses everyday life activities (occupations) to promote health, well-being, and your ability to participate in the important activities in your life. This includes any meaningful activity that a person wants to accomplish, including taking care of yourself and your family, working, volunteering, going to school, among many others. (source: https://www.aota.org/about/what-is-ot)

Palliative Care – specialized medical care for people living with a serious illness, such as cancer or heart failure. Patients in palliative care may receive medical care for their symptoms, along with treatment intended to cure their serious illness. Palliative care is meant to enhance a person's current

# RESOURCES

care by focusing on quality of life. (source: https://www.nia.nih.gov/health/what-are-palliative-care-and-hospice-care)

Primary Care Physician (PCP) – the main doctor you see for regular check-ups, when you are sick, or when you are in need of healthcare services

Pelvic Floor Dysfunction (PFD) – pelvic floor dysfunction is the inability to correctly relax and coordinate your pelvic floor muscles to have a bowel movement. Symptoms include constipation, straining to defecate, having urine or stool leakage, and experiencing a frequent need to pee. (source: https://my.clevelandclinic.org)

Pelvic Floor Physical Therapy (PFPT) – pelvic health therapy involves physical methods of strengthening and or relaxing the muscles of the pelvic floor to help improve core stability and control over urination, bowel movements, and sexual function

Power of Attorney (POA) - gives one or more persons the power to act on your behalf as your agent. The power may be limited to a particular activity or may give temporary or permanent authority to act on your behalf. The power may take effect immediately, or only upon the occurrence of a future event, usually a determination that you are unable to act for yourself due to mental or physical disability. (source: https://www.americanbar.org)

Physician Orders for Life-Sustaining Treatment (POLST) – a physician's order that outlines a plan of end-of-life care reflecting both a patient's preferences concerning care at life's end and a physician's judgment based on a medical evaluation (source: https://www.cedars-sinai.org/programs/healthcare-ethics/polst.html)

Probate – the official proving of a will (source: Oxford Dictionary)

Physical Therapy (PT) – therapy that is used to preserve, enhance, or restore movement and physical function impaired or threatened by disease, injury, or disability, and that utilizes therapeutic exercise, physical modalities (such as massage and electrotherapy), assistive devices, and patient education, and training (source: Merriam-Webster Dictionary)

Registered Nurse (RN) – a nurse who has graduated from a college's nursing program or from a school of nursing and has passed a national licensing exam (Source: Oxford Dictionary)

Skilled Nursing Facility (SNF) – in-patient rehabilitation center that provides 24-hour skilled nursing care

Speech Therapy – used to treat language disorders, speech disorders, and swallowing problems

Trust, Living – a legal document that establishes a trust for any assets you wish to transfer into it and distribute after your death

Trustee – the person responsible for managing the assets in a trust

Veterans Affairs (VA) – provide health, education, disability, funerary, and financial benefits to Veterans of the United States Armed Forces

Will – a legal declaration of a person's wishes as to the disposition of their property or estate after death

Made in the USA
Monee, IL
17 October 2023